BADER
Reading and Language
Inventory

Fourth Edition

Lois A. Bader

Michigan State University

Merrill
Prentice Hall

Upper Saddle River, New Jersey
Columbus, Ohio

Library of Congress Cataloging-in-Publication Data

Bader, Lois A.
    Bader reading and language inventory / Lois A. Bader. — 4th ed.
        p. cm.
    Includes bibliographical references.
    ISBN 0-13-089598-9
    1. Reading—Ability testing.   2. Language arts—Ability testing.   I. Title: Reading and
    language inventory. II. Title.
    LB1050.46.B33   2002
    428′.0076—dc21   00-066427

Vice President and Publisher: Jeffery W. Johnston
Editor: Linda Ashe Montgomery
Production Editor: Mary M. Irvin
Design Coordinator: Diane C. Lorenzo
Project Coordination and Text Design: Carlisle Publisher Services
Cover Design: Rod Harris
Cover Photo: Photo 20/20
Production Manager: Pamela D. Bennett
Director of Marketing: Kevin Flanagan
Marketing Manager: Krista Groshong
Marketing Coordinator: Barbara Koontz

This book was set in Times Roman by Carlisle Communications, Ltd., and was printed and bound by Courier Kendallville, Inc. The cover was printed by Phoenix Color Corp.

Earlier edition © 1983 by Lois Bader

Prentice-Hall International (UK) Limited, *London*
Prentice-Hall of Australia Pty. Limited, *Sydney*
Prentice-Hall Canada, Inc., *Toronto*
Prentice-Hall Hispanoamericana, S.A., *Mexico*
Prentice-Hall of India Private Limited, *New Delhi*
Prentice-Hall of Japan, Inc., *Tokyo*
Prentice-Hall Singapore Pte. Ltd.
Editora Prentice-Hall do Brasil, Ltda., *Rio de Janeiro*

10 9 8 7 6 5 4 3 2
ISBN 0-13-089598-9

PREFACE

To the extent that students' needs are understood, they can be helped to learn. As a result of the dedication of many teachers, specialists, and researchers, a great deal has been learned about factors that influence achievement in basic areas of functioning such as reading, writing, and arithmetic. This knowledge is tempered with the realization that assessment of achievement, as well as the factors underlying achievement, is a complex process requiring conclusions that must be considered tentative. Teachers of children, adolescents, and adults, however, have instructional decisions to make. They need to make referrals to specialists in vision, hearing, and language development, as appropriate, to meet the needs of individual students. Yet most teachers have teaching responsibilities that make individual, in-depth evaluation difficult to do. Most reading and learning specialists have demands on their time, too. Thus, this inventory was developed for teachers and specialists who need a diagnostic battery that encompasses vital areas of evaluation based on research and practice, efficient in administration and interpretation, and relatively inexpensive to use.

Concerns about "high stakes testing" that results in children, teens, and adults being erroneously failed or excluded have been raised repeatedly in the popular media and in professional publications. Professional authorities have long recommended individual tests for children and adults who fail group-administered or pencil-and-paper tests. This inventory provides valid, reliable procedures for individual assessment. The instruments within can assist teachers and specialists to discover inhibiting conditions that can be ameliorated with appropriate instruction.

NEW IN THIS EDITION

The fourth edition of the *Bader Reading and Language Inventory* has been revised to improve its organization, increase its passages' appeal, provide more guidance for subtest selection and sequencing, expand English as a second language record keeping, highlight phonemic and emergent literacy assessment, and provide a model for diagnostic and instructional decision making.

The flowcharts are more accessible. Flowcharts for quick screening, basic assessment, and diagnostic testing are on the inside front cover. A flowchart for preliteracy and emergent literacy is on the inside back cover. Page numbers on the charts provide for easier location of the tests.

An instructor's checklist now supplements the English as a second language screening test. These instruments have been used with thousands of migrant families, refugees, and immigrants in the last eight years and found to be practical, useful, and accurate for initial program placement and for monitoring development in English both by teachers and by tutors.

A case study presented by Michelle Johnston, Ph.D., provides a clear example of the reasoning of a diagnostician as he or she plans and carries out an assessment and makes recommendations for instruction.

Although earlier editions of the inventory contained tests to assess phonemic awareness and emergent literacy, the subtests pertaining to these areas are now highlighted through a revised sequence and with more explanation.

The remainder of the inventory has undergone minor changes based on recommendations of reviewers who are literacy authorities from universities across the nation. These reviewers who have used the inventory report that they are satisfied with its content.

ACKNOWLEDGMENTS

My appreciation is extended to Dr. Michelle Johnston for her case study contribution and her thoughtful suggestions. She is an outstanding professional. I gratefully acknowledge permission to reprint from the following publishers:

Addison-Wesley Publishing Company. Adapted from *Just Awful*, © 1971 by Alma Marshak Whitney, by permission of Addison-Wesley Publishing Company, Inc.

Prentice Hall: *History of a Free People*, 10th Revised Ed., by Henry W. Bragdon and Samuel P. McCutchen. Copyright © 1981 Prentice-Hall, Inc.: *Background for Tomorrow: An American History* by Bertha Davis, Dorothy S. Arnof, and Charlotte Croon Davis, Upper Saddle River: Prentice-Hall, Inc., 1969: SERIES: *Prentice Hall Reading 1980*, Carl B. Smith and Ronald Wardhaugh. Senior Authors, copyright © 1980 Prentice-Hall, Inc., PAST TO PRESENT: A WORLD HISTORY by Sydney H. Zebel and Sidney Schwartz, Copyright © 1960 Prentice Hall, Inc.

The Putnam Publishing Group: Reprinted by permission of Coward, McCann & Geoghegan, Inc. from *The Aquanauts*, copyright © 1971 by Arthur Schaffert.

The H. W. Wilson Company: "Waukewa's Eagle" by James Buckham, published by D. Appleton-Century Company, Inc. in *St. Nicholas Magazine*, copyright © 1900 and 1928, and the version of "Waukewa's Eagle" by Katherine Williams Watson in *Once Upon a Time*. The H. W. Wilson Company, copyright © 1942.

I also thank the following reviewers for their invaluable feedback: Cathy Collins Block, Texas Christian University; Patricia H. Duncan, Virginia Commonwealth University; Larry Kenney, University of Wisconsin–Whitewater; Terry Salinger, International Reading Association; Mary M. Williams, University of San Diego; Barbara J. Erickson, Texas Southern University; Alan M. Frager, Miami University–Ohio; and Kouider Mokhtari, Oklahoma State University.

BRIEF CONTENTS

v

CONTENTS

PART 1

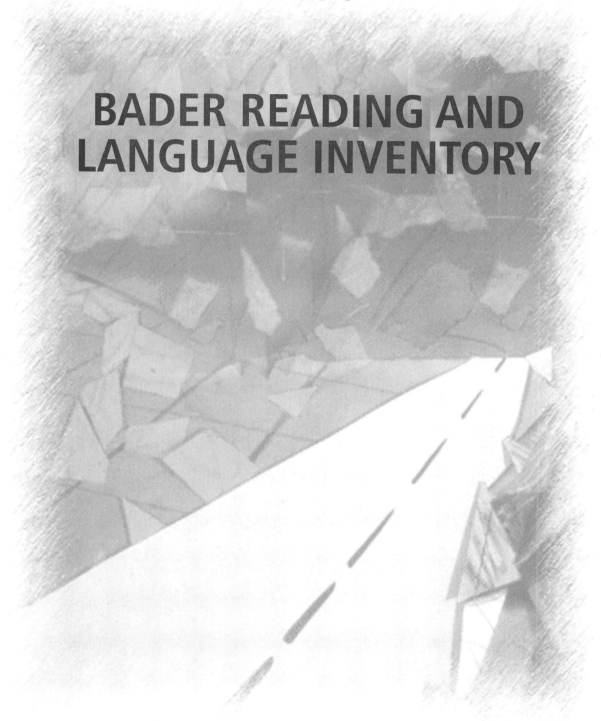

BADER READING AND LANGUAGE INVENTORY

THE BADER READING
AND LANGUAGE INVENTORY

PURPOSE OF THE INVENTORY

The Bader Reading and Language Inventory was constructed for use by literacy specialists, resource teachers, and classroom teachers. The graded passages, the major section of the battery, were designed to determine appropriate placement of students in instructional materials. Additional reasons for administering the inventory include measuring a student's progress, assessing the effectiveness of specific reading approaches, and diagnosing specific literacy difficulties. Because students who experience difficulty in learning to read may have problems in other areas, several informal tests are provided so that their needs and abilities can be assessed. Procedures are suggested for evaluating error quality and quantity because both qualitative and quantitative aspects of performance must be considered. These results can be used for individual and group instructional planning. Portions of the inventory can be used for quick screening or initial placement of students.

ASSESSMENT MODEL

A thorough assessment includes: personal interviews and reflections, observations, informal and formal tests and diagnostic teaching. The Inventory provides several tools and guides for this model. However, the quest for pertinent information should be balanced against the need not to distress the student or take time from instruction by overtesting.

CONTENT OF THE INVENTORY

Graded Reading Passages

The reading passages range from preprimer through twelfth-grade level in difficulty. The passages have been designed to enable the examiner to assess comprehension and word recognition abilities so that the reader's instructional level might be determined.

Three sets of passages have been constructed for each level. The content of the first set has been adapted from the kind of materials used in readers on the primary levels and content-area materials on secondary levels; this set is designated C, for children. The second set has been designed for use with children, adolescents, or adults; it is designated C/A, for children and adults. The third set is intended for use with adults; this set is designated A, for adults, and may also be used with adolescents. The preprimer to third-grade A passages are intended for adults at the beginning reading levels. On the intermediate levels, the adult passages have been designed to assess functional literacy in life-role areas. Beyond the eighth-grade level, all passages have been constructed to assess reading in areas such as history, science, and citizenship.

Word Recognition Lists

Word recognition lists include a graded word list and experiential word lists. The graded word list is a series of 10 words at each level from preprimer through eighth grade plus a list designated as high school. This test was designed to provide an estimate of the reader's level of reading so the examiner can select an entry level to the graded paragraphs. Since the publication of the first edition, numerous test users have reported the reading level estimate of the word list to be highly accurate. In addition, the graded list can serve as a quick check of the student's word recognition and word analysis abilities. Finally, by contrasting the reader's ability to read words in context with word recognition in isolation, the examiner can obtain some information about the reader's ability to use context as an aid to word recognition.

Four experiential word lists are provided: Instructional Directions List, Experience List I, Experience List II, and Functional Literacy List. The first list contains 15 words frequently used in instructional materials and tests. The experience lists each contain 15 words that beginning readers may have learned in daily life. The functional list contains 15 words that may be encountered in completing forms and managing personal affairs in daily life.

English as a Second Language Screening

The English as a Second Language test can be used for initial screening. A list of questions requiring one-word/concrete replies begins the test. Upper-level items require longer replies and give information about student concerns. An English as a second language checklist guides instruction.

Spelling Tests

Seven spelling tests are provided. These may be given selectively to obtain information about the student's abilities in auditory and visual discrimination and memory, cognitive language development, sound-symbol association, and knowledge of spelling conventions. Although the primary use of each test is suggested in the title, additional kinds of information may be obtained. These tests and their levels are:

1. Words with silent letters, P-2
2. Words with silent letters, 3+
3. Words spelled phonetically, P-2
4. Words spelled phonetically, 3+
5. Words illustrating common spelling conventions, 2-4
6. Words illustrating common spelling conventions, 5+
7. Function words commonly misspelled

Preliteracy and Emergent Literacy

Tests are presented to assess the development of prereading skills. While information obtained from these tests is invaluable when testing emergent literacy, a comprehensive evaluation must include additional subtests from the Oral Language, Interest Inventory, and Spelling Tests subsections. The tests in this section include Literacy Awareness, Blending, Segmenting, Letter Knowledge, Hearing Letter Names in Words, and Syntax Matching. Visual and Auditory Discrimination Tests are provided for screening and referral purposes.

Phonics and Structural Analysis

The phonics and structural analysis inventories contain 11 subtests to be given selectively to obtain information pertinent to some areas of knowledge and abilities that may underlie word recognition. These tests include Single Consonants, Consonant Blends, Consonant Digraphs, Vowel Digraphs, Long Vowel Sounds, Short Vowel Sounds, Reversals, Inflectional Suffixes, Derivational Suffixes, Prefixes, and Compound Words.

Cloze Tests

Four cloze tests are included to be used selectively to assess knowledge and abilities in semantic, syntactic, and grammatical processing. These tests may be read to the student or may be read by the student. They are:

- Cloze tests for beginning readers
- Semantic closure
- Syntactic closure
- Grammatical closure

Evaluation of Language Abilities

Instructions for obtaining samples of reader performance in various language areas and checklists for evaluation are provided. Language areas include:

- Oral language expression
- Oral language reception
- Written language expression
- Handwriting

Arithmetic

This test includes a brief test of ability in the areas of addition, subtraction, multiplication, fractions, division, and decimals. A higher score in math than in reading may be a strong indicator of possible reading potential.

Open-Book Reading Assessment

Instructions for constructing open-book reading assessments (OBRAs) are provided to enable teachers to learn more about students' abilities to read academic, workplace, or life-role materials.

ADMINISTERING THE INVENTORY

All materials for administering the various parts of the inventory are contained in this book. Prepare for testing by duplicating score sheets, checklists, and either K-12 or adult summary sheets that will be needed. These may be placed in folders and labeled so that they are readily accessible. Before each testing, assemble a packet of sheets appropriate to the age and anticipated ability range of the student. The inside front and back covers contain sequences and tests for various populations and purposes, e.g., English as a second language, prereading develpment, quick screening, and diagnosis.

The word lists and passages portion of the Reading and Language Inventory provide an initial framework for assessment. Additional tests in the Inventory may be given as needed. Time needed for giving the Inventory depends on the number of passages the student must read before reaching a frustration level and on the number of individual subtests given.

SUGGESTIONS

1. After determining the reading level, decide what additional information regarding the student's skills development and reading processing is necessary for diagnostic teaching. Specify what areas need to be assessed and then select appropriate subtests. Give the student enough individual tests to determine specific weaknesses and patterns of performance. In any one session, the total amount of time spent testing probably should not exceed 30 minutes for primary children or one hour for older students. The primary reason for terminating testing is that the student's level of fatigue or interest has been exceeded.

2. Be efficient. Diagnosis based on a limited quantity of data may result in the examiner drawing erroneous conclusions. The data must be extensive enough to get an accurate account of reading difficulties. However, overextending the diagnosis may prove stressful. Administering additional tests that do not supply useful information could be both unnecessary and counterproductive.

3. Try to create a relaxed atmosphere. This is easily established if testing is done by the classroom teacher in a familiar environment. Problems may arise if the student is placed in a strange situation and tested by an unknown person. Under these circumstances, try to ensure that the student is not uncomfortable because this might affect his/her performance and result in an inaccurate diagnosis.

4. Assess both acquired and deficient skills. Learn about student interests. To improve a student's self-confidence, a remediation program should start with what the student knows. Because a good remedial program focuses initially on strengths, it is imperative to determine what the student's strengths are.

5. Do not overgeneralize the test results by making statements about the student's reading problem that are not based solely on the data obtained. Be careful not to extend the information and supply reasons for the reading problem that may not be accurate. Some examiners are too quick to blame a poor home environment for reading difficulty when the problem actually resulted from other circumstances.

6. Determine the coping strategies of students. When students read orally from either word recognition lists or context, record the specific miscues. This might give insight into the student's patterns of performance and assist in the selection of individual subtests.

7. The informal inventory is particularly helpful for finding the achievement level of students at the extreme reading levels. Those reading either below or above their grade-level placement should be tested in order to determine appropriate placement in materials for instruction. It might also help to test students who are reading on grade level but have a skill deficiency.

TESTING SEQUENCES: FLOWCHARTS

The sequence for administering subtests depends on several factors, including the ability level of the reader, time allotment, and objectives for testing. Select the subtests appropriate for gaining insights into the reader's strengths and weaknesses. Flowcharts with page numbers are provided inside the front and back covers for pre-literacy, K-12 and adult literacy, and quick screening and diagnostic testing. While the charts are provided for the users' convenience, the actual selection and sequence of subtests depends on the individual student and situation.

Give the preliteracy tests to nonreaders and struggling beginning readers who do not score above the preprimer level on the graded word lists and passages. Select subtests primarily from the preliteracy section. Assess metalin-guistic skills by starting with either the language or the print awareness subcategories. The suggested order for ad-ministering these subcategories may be altered according to the individual testing situation. The sequence presented is only one of several valid options but may prove helpful to inexperienced teachers or specialists. Some nonread-ers may be able to complete the easier subtests from Phonics and Word Analysis tests.

Children in the upper grades and teens who are reading on or close to grade level, but struggling in school, should be given an OBRA on content area material most frequently used in their classes. Adults reading on or above the fourth-grade level should be given an OBRA on daily life, workplace, or academic material if they are in school.

In general, start by giving an interest inventory to establish rapport, observe language facility, and determine reader interests. Next, administer the graded word lists to determine a starting point for the graded passages and the supplementary word lists, if appropriate. After administering the graded passages to ascertain the student's reading level, give the spelling tests. Remaining tests may be given as needed.

STUDENT BACKGROUND INFORMATION

Forms are included to assist in the collection of background information, if it is available from home or the classroom teacher. The adult intake information form includes the adult interview and referral information.

Summarizing Assessment

The results of the student evaluation can be summarized on the Bader Reading and Language Inventory Summary Sheet (K-12) (see p. 148) or on the Bader Reading and Language Inventory Summary Sheet (Adult) (see p. 150). The K-12 form contains the following categories: reading profile, including instructional level and needs in reading; language development needs; instructional needs in spelling, handwriting, and arithmetic; visual and auditory difficulties; emergent literacy; student strengths, priorities, interests, and concerns; and recommendations for instruction. The adult form contains information useful in tutoring for basic literacy and English as a second language.

Copies of relevant checklists or subtests of the inventory and other samples of the student's work can be sta-pled to the summary sheet to provide more specific information.

The examiner is encouraged to give as few or as many tests as seem to be appropriate. Finally, she or he should remember that recommendations for instruction should be made on all observations and information available, in-cluding the student's interests and attitudes as well as the instructional assistance that will be available. Whenever possible, trial teaching should be done to verify diagnosis and the selection of appropriate methods. Therefore, this assessment de-emphasizes conclusions drawn from quantification of a few limited samples of behavior. Teachers and reading and learning specialists are encouraged to consider the student's abilities and needs from a holistic perspective.

PART 2

TEST BATTERY

STUDENT PRIORITIES AND INTERESTS

The priorities of the learner are paramount in planning remediation. Not only will learning be more rapid if the student is working in areas of interest and concern, but instructional sessions will also be more pleasant. In addition, students often know the nature of their reading problems and can provide useful diagnostic information.

Select portions of the Student Priorities and Interests Checklists I and II that seem appropriate. Explaining as necessary, read them to, or with, the student. Then reread each section and ask the student what is first in importance, then second, third, and fourth. Priorities Checklists I.1 or I.2 may be used with children or adults on reading levels 1–8. Use I.1 with nonreaders and level 1 readers and I.2 with readers on levels 2–8. Lists I.3 and I.4 can be used to identify topics of interest for younger (I.3) and older (I.3 and I.4) students. If students select a general category such as animals, ask them which animals are of the most interest. Priorities Checklist II is recommended for use with secondary and college students.

The priorities and interests lists can be used with a group by showing a transparency of each page to students who have been provided with their own copies. Later, students can be grouped and regrouped on the basis of specific needs and interests.

The Unfinished Sentences (p. 15) are of most value to get acquainted with younger students. Ask the child to finish each sentence. Demonstrate as necessary. If a response isn't forthcoming on an item, just move on. Quickly jot down a word or two to help you remember the most significant responses so as to maintain spontaneity. After the task is completed, engage the child in discussion of topics that seem important in getting to know him or her and in establishing rapport.

STUDENT PRIORITIES I

I.1 I need specific help with   (OR)   I.2 I need specific help with

A. ____ The letters of the alphabet	A. ____ Short words
B. ____ The sounds for letters of the alphabet	B. ____ Long words
C. ____ Meanings of words	C. ____ Sounds of each letter
D. ____ Remembering what I hear	D. ____ Sounds of letters together
E. ____ Understanding what I hear	E. ____ Reading faster
F. ____ Writing my name	F. ____ Meanings of words
G. ____ Reading street signs	G. ____ Understanding what I read
H. ____ Using the telephone book	H. ____ Remembering what I read
I. ____ Reading directions	I. ____ Remembering what I hear
J. ____ Reading words on food packages	J. ____ Writing notes or letters
K. ____ Reading menus	K. ____ Spelling
L. ____ Reading the *TV Guide*	L. ____ Handwriting
M. ____ Reading related to work	M. ____ How to study
N. ____ Other: _____	N. ____ Other: _____

STUDENT READING INTERESTS

I.3 I would like to be helped to read books on:

____ Adventures	____ TV and movie stars
____ Mysteries	____ Animals
____ Sports	____ Nature
____ Comics	____ Science
____ Humor	____ History
	____ Other: _____

1.4 (continue with older students)

____ Careers	____ Religions/spiritual
____ Want ads	____ Gardening
____ Personal problems	____ Cooking
____ Travel	____ Crafts
____ Romance	____ Mechanics
____ Home repair	____ Carpentry
____ Children's books	____ Sewing/needlework
	____ Other: _____

STUDENT PRIORITIES II

I. I need specific help with:

A. _____ Long words

B. _____ Short sentences

C. _____ Long sentences

D. _____ Punctuation

E. _____ Reading faster

F. _____ Meanings of words

G. _____ Understanding what I read in:

_____ Paragraphs

_____ Short selections (short stories, essays, and so on)

H. _____ Remembering what I read

I. _____ Remembering what I hear

J. _____ Picking out what to remember when I read

K. _____ Paying attention while I'm reading

L. _____ Telling about what I've read

M. _____ Criticizing what I've read

N. _____ Spelling

O. _____ Handwriting

P. _____ Knowing what to say when I'm writing

Q. _____ Knowing how to organize ideas when writing

R. _____ Knowing how to write correctly

S. _____ Writing research papers

T. _____ Taking tests

U. _____ Using the library

V. _____ Doing computer searches

II. I want to study material connected with:

A. The courses I am taking in _____

_____ .

B. My job as a (manual, directories, direction) _____

_____ .

C. My practical needs such as (forms, maps, schedules) _____

_____ .

D. My hobby _____

_____ .

III. I like to read about _____

_____

_____ .

I would like to read about: _____

_____ .

I would like to read:

____ Newspapers   Parts _____

____ Magazines   Kinds _____

____ Short stories   Types _____

____ Fiction   Types _____

____ Nonfiction   Topics _____

____ Comics   Kinds _____

____ Other _____

I hope I can be helped to _____

_____ .

IV. I prefer to work

____ In a small group with a tutor

____ With another student

____ Individually with a tutor

UNFINISHED SENTENCES

1. Sometimes I like to _____.

2. Last summer I _____.

3. I hope I'll never _____.

4. When I read I _____.

5. My friend likes to _____.

6. I often worry about _____.

7. The best thing about school is _____.

8. Someday I want to _____.

9. The person I like best is _____.

10. I wish someone would _____.

11. Learning to read is _____.

12. My favorite television show is _____.

13. The worst thing about school is _____.

14. I have fun when _____.

15. The biggest problem with reading is _____.

16. After school I like to _____.

17. I wish my teacher would _____.

18. My eyes are _____.

19. I would like to be able to read _____.

20. If I had three wishes I would wish for _____

_____

_____.

Notes from follow-up discussion: _____

_____

_____.

ENGLISH AS A SECOND LANGUAGE
(ESL) QUICK START

Tester: _____   Student: _____

Date: _____   Address: _____

Contact Person: _____   _____ Phone: _____

Address: _____   Native Country: _____

_____ Phone: _____   Years of schooling in native country: _____

ESL Level: _____ 0, _____ I, _____ II, _____ III, _____ IV

Directions: Smile. Speak clearly and slowly with normal volume. Stop after the student is unable to respond to 5 questions. All responses must be in spoken English.

Hello, _____. My name is _____ .
          (student)   (tester)

_____

Oral Questions	Correct or Appropriate Responses (+)
1. How are you?	_____
2. What is this? (indicate pencil, cup, or common object)	_____
3. How many fingers? (indicate "4")	_____
4. What color is this? (indicate black, white, or yellow)	_____
5. What day of the week is this?	_____
6. How did you get here today?	_____
7. What is your favorite food?	_____
8. What do you do for fun?	_____
9. What kind of job would you like to have some day? (OR) What kind of games do you like to play?**	_____
*10. Tell me about your family (OR) tell me about your best friend.**	_____
*11. What kind of material do you want to read in English? (OR) What do you like best in school?**	_____
*12. What kind of help you do you want in speaking English? (OR) Tell me about your favorite TV show or movie.**	_____
*13. What kind of help do you want in writing English? (OR) Tell me what you do after school.**	_____
14. (Optional) Is there something you would like to tell me or ask me?	_____

_____

_____

"Thank you, _____ ."
              (student)

*If answers are brief, say "Please tell me more."
**Alternate questions for children.

Correct Responses	ESL Level	Tentative Interpretation
0–2	0	_____ Unable to understand or respond in English
3–5	I	_____ Able to respond to simple questions with one- or two-word answers
6–8	II	_____ Able to respond to questions with simple short phrases or sentences
9–11	III	_____ Able to produce simple discourse
12–14	IV	_____ Able to express ideas in complex sentences with _____ fair or _____ correct structure

Observation: pronunciation is _____ good _____ fair _____ difficult to understand

Comments: _____

_____

_____

_____

_____

_____

_____

_____

_____

Note: This test can serve as one source of information for placement of ESL students or for assistance in planning initial instruction. Teachers and tutors are encouraged to learn about the culture of their students; to obtain as much relevant information as they can from students, student contacts, or translators; and to be flexible in placement and instruction.

ENGLISH AS A SECOND LANGUAGE (ESL) CHECKLIST

Instructions: Check off communication areas and language elements as they are mastered. Topics are defined by examples.

_____ Basic expressions: yes, no, thank you, please, O.K., fine

_____ Greetings: hello, good bye, how are you

_____ Questions: who, where, when, what

_____ Requests: please help me, show me, tell me

_____ Names of people, places, objects

_____ Numbers, colors

_____ Vocabulary: food, restroom, health, shopping, transportation

_____ Letters and sounds of the alphabet

_____ Words for time, order, quantities, size, distance, location

_____ Word order in phrases and sentences

_____ Articles: a, an, the_____ Conjunctions: and, but, either, or

_____ Pronouns: he, she, him, her, it, they, each, myself, our, themselves

_____ Action verbs: run, talk, lift _____ Forms of to be: is, are, was, am

_____ Prepositions: of, to, from, around, into, on, with, under

_____ Adjectives: large, beautiful _____ Adverbs: quickly, beautifully

_____ Context clues to multiple meaning; homonyms: to, too, two

_____ Subject verb agreement: He does / They do; We are / She is

_____ Pronoun antecedent agreement: Maria / she; Men / they

_____ Pronoun case agreement: Subjects: we, they; objects: us, them

_____ Verb tenses: _____ regular: call, called, (have) called _____ Irregular: see, saw, (have) seen; know, knew, (have) known

_____ Compound and complex sentences

_____ Idiomatic language: change of heart; stick around

_____ Proverbs and other cultural referents

_____ Social conversation

_____ Work place conversation

Other:

Additional Assessment: The following parts of the Inventory may be useful in determining student needs and planning instruction: Grammatical Clozure, Oral Language Expression, Oral Language Reception, and Written Language Expression.

Instruction: Although language elements are listed separately, instruction should proceed in a meaningful context such as: role playing, physical responses and language experience. A recommended sequence: begin in context; isolate to teach a specific skill or concept; return to context.

WORD RECOGNITION LISTS

GRADED WORD RECOGNITION LISTS

Purpose

The graded word list test may be used as a starting point in administering the graded reading passages, as a quick estimate of level, or to gain additional insight into the types of word recognition errors made. It may also be used to compare the student's ability to read words in isolation and in context so that information can be obtained about his or her use of syntactic and semantic clues as aids toward recognizing words.

Administration

Some teachers prefer to photocopy the lists and tape them on cards or type the lists on cards that can be laminated. Then a student can be handed the lists one at a time and is not intimidated by the large number of words on a page. If the student reads directly from the page of the test booklet, the use of a book marker may also help focus on each word. Choose the highest list on which you think the student can recognize all the words and give it to the student. Have the examiner's copy of the same list available for recording errors. If the student makes more than two errors on the first list, drop down to a lower-level list until no more than two errors are made. Ask the student to read consecutively higher lists until four or more words are missed. In order to learn more about a student's ability, the examiner may ask her or him to look over words in the next highest list and read the ones known. This procedure is optional for children but recommended for adults.

Some readers may not know the meanings of some of the words, especially if they have English as a second language or a limited background. Informally assess vocabulary by asking students what some of the words mean.

DIRECTIONS: Say, "*Please read these words to me. Try to say them all, even if you are not sure of some of them. Start with this list* (present it to the reader). *Use the book marker if you think it will help you keep your place.*"

RECORDING ERRORS:

   A. ***Entry level for graded reading passages.*** If the only purpose in giving the word list is to estimate reading level or determine a starting point for the graded reading passages, simply record each word read correctly with a check √ and each word read incorrectly or not attempted with a minus (−). Self-corrections would be counted as correct.
   B. ***Diagnostic purposes.*** If the word list is given to gain additional information about the reader's word recognition ability, a more extensive recording system is necessary. If the reader pauses before saying the word, use two checks (√√). Indicate words pronounced incorrectly by using diacritical marks or writing the word as pronounced. If the reader self-corrects, add a *C*. If a word part is omitted, draw a line through it.

Probe vocabulary knowledge by asking the reader to define some of the words. This is especially important for those with English as a second language. Note words the reader cannot define.

SCORING: The student's instructional level is the highest list on which no more than two errors were made. If a student missed only one word, add a half-grade level. For example, if she or he missed one word on the fourth-grade list and three or more words on the fifth-grade list, indicate her level as 4.5. Two words missed on the fourth-grade list would be indicated as 4.0.

INTERPRETATION OF ERRORS: Ascertain additional information about the student's reading by noting whether the error occurs in the beginning, middle, or end of the word. Indicate the letter or letter combination that is mispronounced.

A comparison between the types of reading errors made in and out of context is helpful when determining a student's use of semantic and syntactic cues. For example, if a reader mispronounced the word *where* on the graded word list but read the sentence *Where is my dog?* correctly, the reader used other words in the sentence to recognize the unknown word. In order to correctly guess the word *where,* the student had to have known the remaining words *is my dog* and understood how they interrelate both semantically and syntactically. Additionally, the unknown word must have been in the reader's meaning vocabulary.

Students will usually read more words correctly when they are in context. If a student can pronounce words in a sentence but not on a word list, he or she has probably developed an understanding of the interrelationship of words but may have difficulty with word sound–symbol elements.

GRADED WORD LISTS

Student Name _____ Highest instructional level (2w) _____

A	B	C	D
(PP)	(P)	(1.0)	(2.0)
____ the	____ come	____ today	____ biggest
____ am	____ you	____ does	____ where
____ get	____ went	____ three	____ yourself
____ is	____ him	____ from	____ those
____ and	____ two	____ under	____ before
____ here	____ then	____ began	____ things
____ see	____ know	____ name	____ stopped
____ not	____ around	____ there	____ place
____ can	____ pet	____ could	____ always
____ will	____ house	____ again	____ everyone

E	F	G	H
(3.0)	(4.0)	(5.0)	(6.0)
____ morning	____ important	____ because	____ aircraft
____ since	____ airport	____ bridge	____ necessary
____ together	____ through	____ microscope	____ argument
____ begin	____ fifteen	____ curious	____ chemical
____ which	____ information	____ estimation	____ representative
____ near	____ ocean	____ reliable	____ terminal
____ should	____ preview	____ government	____ apology
____ yesterday	____ laughter	____ business	____ instruction
____ eight	____ preparation	____ direction	____ evidence
____ remember	____ building	____ avenue	____ consideration

GRADED WORD LISTS

I	J	K
(7.0)	(8.0)	(H.S.)
_____ frustration	_____ psychology	_____ geometric
_____ explanation	_____ limitation	_____ molecule
_____ economical	_____ democracy	_____ editorialize
_____ recognition	_____ environment	_____ antecedent
_____ triumphant	_____ barometer	_____ physics
_____ insignificant	_____ prohibited	_____ metaphorical
_____ peculiar	_____ relevance	_____ iniquity
_____ observation	_____ calculate	_____ extenuating
_____ glossy	_____ counselor	_____ succinct
_____ astronomer	_____ endorsement	_____ poignant

GRADED WORD LISTS

A	B
the	come
am	you
get	went
is	him
and	two
here	then
see	know
not	around
can	pet
will	house

C	D
today	biggest
does	where
three	yourself
from	those
under	before
began	things
name	stopped
there	place
could	always
again	everyone

GRADED WORD LISTS

E

morning

since

together

begin

which

near

should

yesterday

eight

remember

F

important

airport

through

fifteen

information

ocean

preview

laughter

preparation

building

G

because

bridge

microscope

curious

estimation

reliable

government

business

direction

avenue

H

aircraft

necessary

argument

chemical

representative

terminal

apology

instruction

evidence

consideration

GRADED WORD LISTS

I	J
frustration	psychology
explanation	limitation
economical	democracy
recognition	environment
triumphant	barometer
insignificant	prohibited
peculiar	relevance
observation	calculate
glossy	counselor
astronomer	endorsement

K

geometric

molecule

editorialize

antecedent

physics

metaphorical

iniquity

extenuating

succinct

poignant

EXPERIENTIAL WORD LISTS

One or more of the experiential word lists may be given at the discretion of the examiner. The Instructional Directions List (A) may be administered to learn whether the student can recognize words frequently encountered in instructional materials and tests. The examiner should ask the reader to describe what the word or phrase means if there is any reason to doubt his or her understanding of these tasks. Students who lack concepts pertaining to these terms may include those who speak English as a second language and those with little experience in formal schooling. The Experience Lists (B and C) may be administered to those students who were unable to read the preprimer level of the graded word list; List I is intended for children, and List II is intended for adults. The examiner may also ask the student what words she or he knows, print them on cards, and after a delay present them in random order. These probes are used to discover whether the student has been able to learn any words frequently encountered in daily life. The Functional Literacy List (D) may be administered to adolescents or adults who appear to be able to read above the third-grade level. Results of the various supplementary lists can serve as departure points for instruction if some words are known. Further assessment may be indicated in visual or auditory acuity and discrimination or vocabulary.

Research on emergent literacy (Bader and Hildebrand, 1992) focused on children's "reading" of logos, such as *McDonald's* and *Burger King.* Color logos were cut from magazines and presented to the children for identification. Later they were asked to read the words in type. Little transfer occurred. Only the words *stop* and *Kmart* were recognized in logo and type. They were the most similar in both forms. Diagnosticians may wish to use logos prominent in the environment of their children and adults to examine this capability as they test for word recognition. Functionally illiterate adults often tell us they don't try to read signs.

EXPERIENTIAL WORD LISTS

A

INSTRUCTIONAL DIRECTIONS LIST

____ circle   ____ name

____ match   ____ outline

____ cross out   ____ shade

____ underline   ____ list

____ label   ____ complete

____ connect   ____ number

____ mark   ____ fill in the blank

____ trace

B

EXPERIENCE LIST I (Children)

____ stop   ____ push

____ keep out   ____ walk

____ danger   ____ park

____ McDonald's   ____ pull

____ boys   ____ ice cream

____ school   ____ Pepsi-Cola

____ girls   ____ go

____ exit

C

EXPERIENCE LIST II (Adult)

____ open   ____ out

____ coffee   ____ stairs

____ warning   ____ help wanted

____ for rent   ____ do not cross

____ police   ____ hospital

____ one way   ____ for sale

____ bus stop   ____ no smoking

____ hot dog   ____ license

D

FUNCTIONAL LITERACY LIST

____ address   ____ prescription

____ telephone   ____ occupation

____ references   ____ social security

____ poison   ____ registration

____ entrance   ____ emergency

____ cashier   ____ prohibited

____ employee   ____ deductions

EXPERIENTIAL WORD LISTS

A	B
circle	stop
match	keep out
cross out	danger
underline	McDonald's
label	boys
connect	school
mark	girls
trace	exit
name	push
outline	walk
shade	park
list	pull
complete	ice cream
number	Pepsi-Cola
fill in the blank	go

EXPERIENTIAL WORD LISTS

C	D
open	address
coffee	telephone
warning	references
for rent	poison
police	entrance
one way	cashier
bus stop	employee
hot dog	prescription
out	occupation
stairs	social security
help wanted	registration
do not cross	emergency
hospital	prohibited
for sale	deductions
no smoking	
license	

GRADED READING PASSAGES

READING AND LISTENING LEVELS

The major objective in using the graded passages is to estimate the reader's instructional level for placement in materials. The instructional level is defined as the level on which a learner is challenged but not frustrated. Accuracy in word recognition and comprehension are taken into consideration. The examiner is given the option of having the student read aloud, at sight, after a brief introduction, or silently before reading aloud. These conditions are termed *unprepared* and *prepared* reading

Grade Levels Primer—Third

Accuracy		Comprehension
Prepared oral reading: 95%	Unprepared oral reading: 90%	Depending on detail, memories: 60–70%

Grade Levels Fourth and Above

Accuracy		Comprehension
Prepared: 98%	Unprepared: 95%	Depending on detail, memories: 60–70%

The three sets of graded passages (C, C/A, A) are to be used to obtain an instructional reading level based on responses after oral and silent reading. An instructional *listening* level can also be obtained—by evaluating responses of the student after hearing passages read aloud by the examiner. The minimum level of memories after listening is 60% for instructional level.

The 60% figure under "Comprehension" does not mean the reader understands only 60% of what was read or heard. Rather, this figure refers to a percentage of ideas recalled, mostly literal details, and represents a higher level of comprehension than 60%, according to research.

It seems reasonable to assume that more difficult materials will usually result in frustration for the student and that easier materials can be read by the student independently of teacher support. Therefore, the examiner is not burdened with percentages for these level designations. Understanding and recall for specific passages are affected by the background and interest of the reader. These factors must be considered when estimating the ability of a particular student to comprehend various materials.

Examiners do not have to compute percentages. An Instructional Level Guide is provided with each passage.

DETERMINING A STARTING POINT

Results from either the graded word list test or from school records are used to determine a starting point for the graded passages. Within each level, choose the passage—designated for children (C), children or adults (C/A), or adults (A)—that appears to be most suited to the reader, regardless of age. What is most important is to choose a passage that the reader might find the most interesting or appealing. Select the highest-level passage that the student would appear to be able to read independently. If school records, for example, indicate that a student is having moderate difficulty reading fifth-grade-level material, start the graded passages at a second-grade level. If the selected passage is too difficult, move down until the independent level is found. Proceed with more difficult material until the student reaches a frustration level.

If information about level of functioning is absent, administer the graded word list test. Have the student begin reading the graded passages one level below the highest level on which no more than two words were missed on the graded word list test, or the highest independent level. If a student, for example, missed one word on the first-, second-, and third-grade lists and two words on the fourth-grade lists, start the graded passages at the third-grade level. Have the student continue reading more advanced graded passages until the frustration level is reached.

ORAL READING

Unprepared versus Prepared Oral Reading

The unprepared oral reading condition can save time during testing and can give the examiner information on the reader's ability to instantly recognize words and process ideas. However, some students have difficulty in oral expression and need an opportunity to read silently before reading aloud in order to give a more accurate display of their abilities to recognize words. Either condition may be used at the examiner's discretion.

DIRECTIONS FOR ORAL PASSAGES: In each form, the Examiner's Copy will include a statement to assess the reader's background knowledge and a motivating statement. For both unprepared and prepared oral reading, first read the title of the passage to the student. Next, read the prepared statement to assess the reader's background knowledge. If background knowledge appears inadequate, select an alternative passage from a different form.

Unprepared Oral Reading.   Say to the student, *"Here are some passages I would like you to read. Please read this one aloud. Try to remember what you read so that you might be able to tell me about it or answer questions about the passage."* Finally, read the motivating statement that accompanies each passage to develop a purpose for reading.

Prepared Oral Reading.   Say, *"Here are some passages I would like you to read. Please read this one silently to yourself. Tell me when you have finished; then I will have you read it to me. Try to remember what you read so that you might be able to tell me about it or answer questions about the passage."* Finally, read the motivating statement that accompanies each passage to develop a purpose for reading.

As the student reads aloud, record her or his performance by using the code in this section or a code that is familiar to you. Check appropriate blanks with regard to meaningful word substitutions and rate. The kinds of oral reading inaccuracies, if they are numerous, may be marked after the student has departed. Repeat this procedure with higher-level passages until the student has failed to meet the minimum requirements for oral reading accuracy as indicated at the end of each passage page.

RECORDING AND SCORING ORAL READING PERFORMANCE

Miscues (oral reading errors) can be evaluated both quantitatively and qualitatively. In order to determine the reading levels quickly, we recommend a quantitative analysis that gives consideration to evidence of frustration. Miscues will be analyzed qualitatively later to assist in remediation procedures.

A quantitative analysis focuses on the number of miscues, or deviations from the printed text. These include substitutions, insertions, omissions, repetitions, words unknown, dialect, and self-corrections. As the student reads aloud, record his or her performance, count the miscues, and use the total to determine the student's reading level.

If a tape recorder is available and the reader is not disturbed by being taped, tape the student's reading, and check her or his accuracy by coding performance at a later time.

The major purpose of making a record of performance during oral reading is to analyze the reader's strengths and difficulties as he or she attempts to use oral language in extracting meaning from printed language. Therefore, all deviations from the texts are to be recorded even though they may not be considered as errors.

With the exception of beginning readers, most students will have better comprehension after silent reading than after oral reading. The purpose of oral reading is to ascertain the student's strengths and weaknesses in oral reading miscues. Therefore, for most students reading beyond the primary level, comprehension assessment may be omitted after oral reading. Conversely, students reading below the third-grade level may have better comprehension after oral reading. Giving an oral reading and a silent reading passage at every level can be time-consuming and stressful for the student but may be done at the examiner's discretion.

When the frustration level is reached for oral reading (one level above the highest instructional level), begin silent reading with an alternative passage on the student's highest instructional level during oral reading.

The following code and scoring guidelines are recommended.

Code and Scoring Guidelines
of Graded Reading Passages

Behavior	Coding	Example	Scoring
1. Substitutions and mispronunciations that disrupt meaning	Write the response above the word	*gaged* she gazed at it	1
2. Substitutions, mispronunciations, and inversions that do not disrupt meaning	Write the response above the word; draw curved line for inversions	*looked* she gazed at it	0
		"I saw him," Mary said.	0
3. Repeated substitutions or mispronunciations for the same word	Write response each time, but count one error	*wafer* the water was . . . then the *wafer* water flowed	1
4. Insertions	Write the word with a caret	*little* a ∧ dog	1
5. Omissions and partial omissions	Draw a line through word or word part omitted	the ~~tall~~ girl	1
		walki~~ng~~ on	1
6. Words pronounced by the examiner	Wait at least five seconds; write *P* above aided word	P I thought	1
7. Repetitions of words or phrases	Write *R* above each repetition; draw a line over the words repeated; score as 1 regardless of repetitions	R R the cat howled	1

Record but do not score the following:

Behavior	Coding	Example	Scoring
8. Self-corrections	Write C above corrections	C went I want to	0
9. Repetitions to make corrections	As above	C I want to went I want to	0
10. Hesitations	Put a check above each hesitation	√ He thought	0
11. Substitutions and mispronunciations resulting from a dialect	Write the deviation from the text, if there is time	be goin She goes every day	0
12. Ignored punctuation	Put an X over disregarded punctuation	the car ✗ Then	0
13. Phrasing	Insert lines to indicate phrasing, if there is time	the / car / came down the street	0

In the sentence "*She gazed at it,*" the student substituted *gaged* for *gazed* in example one and *looked* for *gazed* in example two. Since *gaged* and *gazed* have very different meanings, the meaning of the sentence is changed. However, the substitution of *looked* for *gazed* does not distort the meaning of the passage. Therefore, the reading behavior in example one is scored one point, while the reading behavior in example two is scored a zero.

In example three, the reader substitutes the word *wafer* for *water* twice in the same passage. Because both incorrect responses are identical, the examiner counts only one miscue, not two. Count consistent mispronunciations of a word several times in a passage only once.

Occasionally a student may omit several words together or even an entire line. If this occurs, count the omission as only one miscue.

SILENT READING AND LISTENING COMPREHENSION

DIRECTIONS: **Silent Reading.** As with oral reading, assess the student's background knowledge. If adequate, say to the student, "*Now I will ask you to read passages silently and then tell me what you have read or answer questions about what you read.*" Continue by reading the motivating statement to the student. When the student has finished, take the passage from him or her.

Comprehension should be assessed after silent reading by using unprompted memories, direct questions, or a combination. With unprompted memories the student retells all the information remembered about the passage. Encourage the student to continue by asking such general questions as, "*Can you think of something else? What else happened? Tell me more.*" Also probe by asking a specific question related to the student's response. When a reader, for example, answers, "The bird was brought in for the little girl to care for," ask, "*What did the little girl do then?*" or, "*What happened to the bird?*" When probing, be certain not to supply the reader with any information that is contained in the passage.

The advantage of unprompted memories is that some readers prefer to tell what they remember rather than be asked pinpointed questions. As they retell the passage, they may remember other facts through association. If students are asked initially to answer questions and are unable to remember, they may become nervous. By asking the student to recall anything remembered about the passage, the examiner is starting with the student's strengths.

Students who have difficulty processing, retrieving, and organizing the information from the passage may require direct questioning. In actual practice, using a combination of unprompted memories and direct questioning is probably best for assessing comprehension. Start by asking the student to simply retell the passage. Continue with general probing questions. Finally, note any missing information and use direct questioning to ascertain whether the student has difficulty retrieving or comprehending the material.

List the memories that are accurately recalled as they occur (i.e., 1-2-3, etc.). On the lower-level passages, a list of possible unprompted memories is supplied with the comprehension questions. On the upper-level passages, use the answers to the questions as a guide, and list order of memories in front of the questions answered. Use the questions to prompt recall of information not given in retelling if the number of recalled memories is inadequate. When the total number of memories from retelling and/or questioning equals the number required on the guide, stop questioning. Retelling, or answers that paraphrase the meaning or wording of the passage, are to be considered correct. As a further probe of the student's ability, the examiner may permit the reader to reinspect the passage to find the answer to a question. Note whether the reader can scan to find information. The interpretive questions are not counted in the total number of memories. If the first passage is too difficult, go to a lower-level passage. Continue with the silent reading of higher-level passages until the student cannot meet the minimum requirements for silent reading comprehension.

Listening Comprehension. Say to the student, *"Now I will read passages to you. Please listen so that you can tell me what you heard or answer questions about what you heard."* Begin with an alternative passage on the highest instructional level achieved under the silent reading procedure, and continue reading aloud higher-level passages until the student cannot meet the minimum requirements for listening comprehension.

INTERPRETING AND SUMMARIZING THE RESULTS OF THE GRADED PASSAGES

To convert the raw score into a reading level, the teacher should consult the Instructional Level Guide at the bottom of the Examiner's Copy of each graded passage. Separate limits are available for both prepared and unprepared oral reading. Select the limit for the appropriate circumstance, and compare that figure to the total number of miscues the reader made. If the total number of miscues is within the designated limit, the student has not reached the instructional level. Continue having the student read until the frustration level for word recognition is determined.

The student's highest instructional level for word recognition is used as a starting point for comprehension assessment. After the student has read the passage silently, count the total number of both prompted and unprompted memories. Compare this total to the criteria established in each instructional level guide. If the number of memories matches or exceeds the limit established, continue having the student read more difficult passages silently until the highest instructional level for comprehension is reached. Many readers have better recall of narrative passages than of expository passages. Performance on both types of passages may be evaluated if time permits.

Record the highest instructional levels achieved by the student on the Summary Sheets under *Reading profile,* oral, silent, and listening designations. Examine the scoring sheets and consider all of the reading behaviors of the student. A great deal can be inferred about comprehension from oral reading. A lack of inflection, word-by-word reading, or inappropriate inflection and emphasis may indicate poor comprehension. Inappropriate substitutions, in particular, may indicate difficulties, whereas good substitutions indicate the converse. It is well to remember, however, that these are inferences. Some flat, word-by-word oral readers are competent in comprehension.

Generally, the student's instructional level should be the highest-level passage in which there is adequate comprehension in silent reading. However, if the student's reading is extremely slow, the instructional level may be one level lower than the passage on which comprehension was adequate. The term *instructional level* as used here refers to an instructional condition in which the teacher is giving direct aid, support, and guidance. In some instructional settings, students are expected to work independently of the teacher; they may be asked to read and answer questions, complete worksheets, or follow directions without assistance. This is termed *independent learning level* and should be about one level below the instructional level for levels P–5 and two levels below for 6–12. Estimation of the independent learning level should only be made by someone familiar with the instructional program in which the student will be placed.

The listening comprehension level may be used as an estimate of current potential and indicates the student's capacity for understanding what is heard.

To a great extent, teacher judgment is required in placing students in materials because many factors beyond word recognition and comprehension are important. For example, a student may be given some easy materials to read for a time in order to build fluency, rate, or confidence. Conversely, a student may be permitted to proceed in difficult materials because of a strong interest in the content. Stages of reading development, age, interests, learning rate, and personality are all factors that may need to be considered as a teacher chooses between the hazards of frustrating a student with difficult materials and not challenging her or him by using easy materials.

In addition to the determination of level or levels of placement, the reader's performance on the graded passages can be analyzed as to strengths and weaknesses to be considered in planning instruction. The Summary Sheets contain checklists where information from graded passages, word lists, phonics, and other tests can be combined and recommendations made for instruction.

EXAMPLE OF TESTING FOR INSTRUCTIONAL LEVEL

(Jeff, a fourth-grade student)

1. Graded Word List: missed 1 word, 1.0
   missed 1 word, 2.0
   missed 5 words, 3.0
   GWL level: 2.5

2. Unprepared Oral Reading

   2C/A—3, score: 1 repetition
   2 substitutions that did change meaning
   2 substitutions that did not change meaning

   Rate appeared to be average. Answer to interpretive question: "Well, this was probably one of those import-type places where the owner was Greek and kept Greek food and things for other Greek people and people who like Greek food. He walked a long way and didn't know where he was."

   3C/A—14, score: 5 mispronunciations that disrupted meaning
   3 words pronounced by examiner
   4 substitutions that disrupted meaning
   2 insertions

   Rate appeared to be slow; many long pauses. Answer to interpretive question: "I guess they like to be famous, and they see neat things."

3. Silent Reading

   2A—Retelling: 8 memories, in sequence
   (80%) no additional memories from questioning

   Rate appeared to be average. Answer to interpretive question: "She probably was a dropout and wants to finish. My brother went to school like that."

   3A—Retelling: 8 memories, in sequence
   (100%) $\underline{+2}$ memories from questioning
   10

Rate appeared to be average. Answer to interpretive question: "If there wasn't a wrong number, they wouldn't know where he moved to."

4A—Retelling: 4 memories, not in sequence
(50%) $\underline{+1}$ memory from questioning
                5

Rate appeared to be slow. Much whispering, making faces. Answer to interpretive question: "Well, if you are rich, you are the best."

Instructional level: 3 (highest instructional level in silent reading)

4. Listening

Ordinarily the examiner would start with an instructional-level passage (3), but since Jeff appeared to have good language development, he was given a passage on the fourth level.

4C—Retelling: 7 memories, in sequence
(80%) $\underline{+1}$ memory from questioning
                8

Answer to interpretive question: "It makes you mad at yourself when you can't do things. I get like that."

5C—Retelling: 7 memories, in sequence
(70%)   no additional memories from questioning

Answer to interpretive question: "Sometimes they can tell you're their friend. You can't trust wild animals, though."

(Jeff did not reach frustration in listening until the seventh-grade level.)

5. Recommended instructional level for materials placement: 3.0
Independent learning level in reading materials: 2.0–2.5
Frustration level: 4.0
Current potential: 6.0

QUALITATIVE ANALYSIS: ANALYSIS AND REMEDIATION FOR GRAPHO-PHONIC, SYNTACTIC, AND SEMANTIC MISCUES

How are student errors analyzed?

Interpret students' reading errors both quantitatively and qualitatively. Quantitative analysis describes a student's reading performance numerically and focuses on the total number of correct and incorrect responses. It is particularly useful for the examiner when determining reading level. However, in order to gain information required for planning appropriate reading instruction, it is necessary to proceed further and analyze the test results qualitatively. Knowing a student's strengths and weaknesses in relation to reading for meaning is essential for planning an effective remediation program.

What is qualitative analysis?

According to Goodman (1969), the quality of reading responses should be analyzed in terms of the reader's reliance on three cue systems: grapho-phonic, syntactic, and semantic cues.

How do the cue systems differ?

Grapho-phonic cues refer to the relationship between the grapheme (letter) and the phoneme (smallest unit of sound). If the word *horse* is substituted for *house,* the reader is using grapho-phonic elements of the text, because the words look and sound similar. If, however, the word substituted was *cabin* for *house,* the reader would not be using grapho-phonic cues, because there is no sound-symbol similarity between the two words.

Syntactic cues are obtained from the grammar of the language. If the sentence "I fed the dog" was read "I bought the dog," the reader is using syntactic cues. By correctly substituting a verb, the reader shows an understanding of the language. If, however, the same sentence is read "I friend the dog," syntactic cues are not being used because the reader incorrectly substitutes a noun for a verb. In this example, the reader finds the material too difficult to use knowledge of language structure.

Semantic cues are derived from the meaning of the sentence. They are obtained from the semantic content of what is read. If the sentence "I feel great" was read "I feel terrific," the reader used semantic cues and is on his or her way to being successful. Semantic cues would not have been used if the same sentence were read "I feel bad." The reader missed the idea of the author; therefore, the substitution did not keep the original meaning of the sentence.

When a reader uses known words in a sentence to help recognize an unknown word, he or she is relying on semantic or syntactic cues. It is impossible to use semantic cues without using syntactic cues. If the substitution is semantically correct, it must also be syntactically correct. However, the reverse does not apply. It is possible for a substitution to be syntactically but not semantically correct. An example of this would be substituting the word *built* for *bought* in the sentence, "I bought a bicycle."

What are the steps involved in a qualitative analysis?

A qualitative analysis is predicated on administering an Informal Reading Inventory (IRI) and attending to the cue system of the student. In order for the examiner to focus on patterns of performance and types of miscues, the student must orally read passages of varying difficulty.

How may oral reading performance indicate a student's reading strategy?

Summarizing all oral reading miscues on a master sheet will yield specific information about students' reading strategies as well as strengths and weaknesses. The following questions, encompassing the three cue systems, should serve as a guide:

1. Does the reader use grapho-phonic strategies?
2. Which specific grapho-phonic elements are known? Which ones are unknown?
3. Is word length related to accuracy? Does the student pronounce a grapho-phonic element correctly in small words but not in larger ones?
4. Are miscues made in the beginning, middle, or end of the word?

5. Is the problem with structural analysis? What specific prefixes and suffixes are known? Which ones are unknown?
6. Can the student use context clues to figure out unknown words?
7. Does the reader have difficulty with particular grammatical functions (verb, adverb, noun)?
8. Does the miscue interfere with comprehension?
9. Is the sentence containing the miscue semantically acceptable, or is there a change in meaning?
10. Does the reader correct the miscue and make the sentence semantically acceptable?
11. What are the most common patterns of performance?

How does the analysis of student errors serve as a guide for remediation?

After answering these questions, make a list of the student's known strengths and weaknesses. Maintain an accounting of the student's knowledge by recording both the text and the miscue. Note whether each miscue is graphically or phonetically similar in the beginning, middle, or end of the original word. Then determine if the miscue is either syntactically or semantically acceptable. Analyze a number of miscues to find a pattern of performance. Our example (see Chart I, p. 40) indicates that the reader uses grapho-phonic cues, especially in the beginning and end of the word. Of the miscues, only two are syntactically and none semantically correct. Consequently, we can conclude that the reader is not using context. The remediation program should address this area of weakness. To design remedial lessons, directly translate this information into instructional objectives. Remedial lessons that start with the strengths and proceed to the teaching of new skills are more meaningful to students. For example, when teaching grapheme-phoneme and structural analysis relationships, it is advantageous to start with words known by sight because students can already relate to them. As new skills are mastered, adjust the list of strengths and weaknesses for each student so that the evaluation remains current.

Is there a recommended strategy for remediation of grapho-phonic cues?

One successful strategy is the inductive teaching of grapho-phonic elements. We recommend the following procedure:

Objective: Grapheme-Phoneme Relationship of *bl*

1. Determine that the prerequisite skills of auditory and visual discrimination have been acquired.
2. Select several words that the students already know by sight that contain the grapho-phonic element to be taught. Write the words in a column. Have the students read the words.

> blue
> blend
> blanket
> blank

3. Ask the students, "*How are all these words alike?*" The students must establish two things: They all start with *bl* letters. They all start with the sound one hears at the beginning of *bl*ack.
4. Read the words to the students while they listen for the letters that represent the /bl/ sound.
5. Ask the students to think of additional words that start with the same sound they hear in *blue, blend, blanket,* and *blank.* Write these additional words under *blank* (the final word on the list).
6. Have students read all the words in the list. Direct them to look at the first two letters and note the beginning sound of the word.
7. To apply the sound-symbol association, students must know the sound the letters represent and be able to blend it with other sounds to produce an entire word. To teach students to blend, begin with a known phonogram (*ake, ack, ink*). If necessary, teach the phonogram by sight. Then place the *bl* in front of the phonogram and have the student pronounce the new word.
8. Students must have the opportunity to practice their new skill in reading. Give students appropriate reading material (instructional level) and have them circle and read all the words that begin with *bl.*

CHART I: QUALITATIVE ANALYSIS OF MISCUES

Miscue	Text	Graphically Similar	Phonetically Similar	Beginning	Middle	End	Syntactically Acceptable	Semantically Acceptable
wanted	waited	✓	✓	✓		✓	✓	
here	her	✓	✓	✓	✓			
change	charge	✓	✓	✓		✓		
round	rigid	✓		✓		✓		
rinsed	rushed	✓		✓		✓	✓	
turn	train	✓	✓	✓		✓		
Summary:		6	4	6	1	5	2	0

What strategies aid students' use of semantic and syntactic cues?

One reason students ignore semantic and syntactic cues is because the material is too difficult. If vocabulary, sentence structure, and concepts are incomprehensible, the reader will be unable to use context effectively. Consequently, the first task is to see if easier or more interesting material corrects the problem. If these adjustments work, it is imperative to provide the students practice time with reading material that is on the appropriate level and matches their interests. However, if students continue to make substitutions that do not keep the meaning of the sentence, proceed with instruction in simple cloze activities. Make students aware of the language's syntactic and semantic cue systems by giving them the following activities:

1. Place a paragraph written on the student's independent reading level on the overhead. Select one part of speech, such as a verb, and cover several verbs in the paragraph with a slip of paper.
2. Proceed with one verb at a time, and discuss with students additional words that fit in the blank and maintain the meaning of the sentence.
3. Place several student responses on the overhead, and discuss whether or not they are appropriate. Focus on how the other words in the same sentence supply cues.
4. Emphasize that cues may be obtained from other sentences and paragraphs.
5. Continue the practice with other parts of speech. Initially implement the activities using teacher-directed, whole-group lessons. Eventually use cooperative student groups. These same types of activities can be used individually when students are silently reading.

REFERENCES

Goodman, K. S. (1969). "Analysis of Reading Miscues: Applied Psycholinguistics." *Reading Research Quarterly, 5,* 9–30.

Goodman, Y. M., Watson, D. J., & Burke, C. L. (1987). *Reading Miscue Inventory: Alternative Procedures.* New York: Richard C. Owen.

GRADED PASSAGES

Passages were developed for children (C) in or near the grade-level designations spanning preprimer (PP) through twelfth grade. Passages written for children or adults are designated C/A. Passages written for adults are designated A. Regardless of designation, select passages best suited for your students.*

The Examiner's Copies are intended for duplication.

Grade-Level Designation	Age Designation	Passage Title	Page No. of Examiner's Copy	Page No. of Reader's Copy'
PP	C	Tip the Cat	42	1
PP	C/A	On the Bus	43	2
PP	A	The Dog Show	44	3
P	C	Lee's Friendly Meal	45	4
P	C/A	Turtles at Home	46	5
P	A	A Slippery Sidewalk	47	6
1	C	Pat and the Kitten	48	7
1	C/A	Tony and the Flower Shop	49	8
1	A	Give Me Room	50	9
2	C	The Song of Little Frog	51	10
2	C/A	Sam Buys a Newspaper	52	11
2	A	Linda at the Diner	53	12
3	C	James' Cut	54	13
3	C/A	Today's Explorers	55	14
3	A	The Lucky Wrong Number	56	15
4	C	Checkers Game for Kim	57	16
4	C/A	The Recovery	58	17
4	A	Land of Many Riches	59	18
5	C	Waukewa's Eagle	60	19
5	C/A	The Nile Valley	61	20
5	A	Not in the Mood to Read	62	21
6	C	Early Tools	63	22
6	C/A	Constellations	64	23
6	A	Driver's Licenses	65	24
7	C	Volcanoes	66	25
7	C/A	Questions about Dinosaurs	67	26
7	A	The Job Application	68	27
8	C	*Kon-Tiki*	69	28
8	C/A	A Shopping Trip	70	29
8	A	A New Job	71	30
9–10	C	Modern Chemistry	72	31
9–10	C/A	A Failure to Communicate	73	32
9–10	A	Voter Drive	74	33
11–12	C	Impressionists	75	34
11–12	C/A	Global Warfare	76	35
11–12	A	Improvement for Workers	77	36

*The number of expository passages increases with level of difficulty for all categories.

GRADED PASSAGE (PPC)

Assessing and Activating Background Knowledge

Here is a story about a cat. What do cats like to do?

_____ Adequate   _____ Inadequate

Motivating Statement   *Read to find out what kind of a pet this is and what things it likes to do.*

TIP THE CAT

Tip is a cat.

She likes to eat fish.

She is a fat cat.

Tip eats fish and sleeps.

She likes to sit on my lap.

She is a good pet.   (31 words)

Unprompted Memories	**Comprehension Questions**
Please retell the story.	_____ *What kind of animal is the story about?* (cat)
_____ cat	_____ *What is the animal's name?* (Tip)
_____ named Tip	_____ *What does Tip eat?* (fish)
_____ likes fish	_____ *What does Tip do?* (eats)
_____ fat cat	_____ (sleeps)
_____ sleeps and eats fish	_____ *Where does Tip like to sit?* (lap)
_____ sits on lap	_____ *What kind of pet is Tip?* (good)
_____ good pet	

Interpretive question: *Why do you think Tip is fat?*

     Acceptable answer: _____ Yes _____ No

Memories: _____ Unprompted + _____ Prompted = _____ Total

Organized retelling: _____ Yes _____ No

Oral reading inaccuracies changed meaning: _____ Yes _____ No

Rate appropriate: _____ Yes _____ No   Fluency appropriate: _____ Yes _____ No

    _____ reads word by word   _____ reads in phrases   _____ good use of punctuation

    _____ good use of stress, pitch, and intonation

Oral reading:

    _____ Substitutions   _____ Mispronunciations

    _____ Additions   _____ Repetitions

    _____ Omissions   _____ Words pronounced by examiner

INSTRUCTIONAL LEVEL GUIDE   Prepared: 2 or fewer errors   Unprepared: 3 or fewer errors   5 or more memories

GRADED PASSAGE (PPC/A)

Assessing and Activating Background Knowledge

Here is a story about some people on a bus. What is it like for you to ride on a bus?

_____ Adequate   _____ Inadequate

Motivating Statement   *Read the story to find out about a bus ride.*

ON THE BUS

We are going home.

Stop and go.

Stop and go.

The bus is so slow.

Look at that man.

He has a bike.

He can go fast.   (27 words)

Unprompted Memories   **Comprehension Questions**
Please retell the story.   _____ *Where were people going?*   (home)

_____ we are going home   _____ *How was the bus traveling?*   (stop and go or slow)

_____ stop and go, stop and go   _____ *What did the people on the bus look at?*   (a man)

_____ look at that man   _____ *What did the man have?*   (a bike)

_____ has a bike   _____ *How was the man traveling?*   (on a bike, or fast)

_____ can go fast

Interpretive question: *Why is the bus so slow?*

_____ Acceptable answer: _____ Yes _____ No

Memories: _____ Unprompted + _____ Prompted = _____ Total

Organized retelling: _____ Yes _____ No

Oral reading inaccuracies changed meaning: _____ Yes _____ No

Rate appropriate: _____ Yes _____ No   Fluency appropriate: _____ Yes _____ No

_____ reads word by word   _____ reads in phrases   _____ good use of punctuation

_____ good use of stress, pitch, and intonation

Oral reading:

_____ Substitutions   _____ Mispronunciations

_____ Additions   _____ Repetitions

_____ Omissions   _____ Words pronounced by examiner

INSTRUCTIONAL LEVEL GUIDE   Prepared: 1 or fewer errors   Unprepared: 3 or fewer errors   3 or more memories

GRADED PASSAGE (PPA)

Assessing and Activating Background Knowledge

This is a story about a dog show. Tell me what you know about dog shows.

    ____ Adequate   ____ Inadequate

Motivating Statement   *Read the story to find out about the different dogs at the dog show.*

THE DOG SHOW

I went to a dog show.

I saw big dogs.

I saw little dogs.

I saw dogs with long hair.

I saw dogs with short hair.

There were dogs everywhere.   (30 words)

Unprompted Memories	**Comprehension Questions**
Please retell the story.	____ *Where did the person go?* (dog show)
____ dog show	____ *What size were the dogs?* (big)
____ big dogs	____ (little)
____ little dogs	____ *What was their hair like?* (long)
____ long hair	____ (short)
____ short hair	____ *Where were the dogs?* (everywhere)
____ everywhere	

Interpretive question: *Why do you think people go to dog shows?*

    Acceptable answer: ____ Yes   ____ No

Memories: ____ Unprompted + ____ Prompted = ____ Total

Organized retelling: ____ Yes ____ No

Oral reading inaccuracies changed meaning: ____ Yes ____ No

Rate appropriate: ____ Yes ____ No   Fluency appropriate: ____ Yes ____ No

    ____ reads word by word   ____ reads in phrases   ____ good use of punctuation

    ____ good use of stress, pitch, and intonation

Oral reading:

    ____ Substitutions   ____ Mispronunciations

    ____ Additions   ____ Repetitions

    ____ Omissions   ____ Words pronounced by examiner

INSTRUCTIONAL LEVEL GUIDE   Prepared: 1 or fewer errors   Unprepared: 3 or fewer errors   4 or more memories

GRADED PASSAGE (PC)

Assessing and Activating Background Knowledge

Here is a story about a fish. What do you know about fish?

_____ Adequate   _____ Inadequate

Motivating Statement   *Read about this special fish and find out what he does and how he lives.*

LEE'S FRIENDLY MEAL

Lee was a little blue fish.

Some of his friends were very big fish.

Lee's big friends lived far away.

But he saw them every day.

Every day they would swim by to see Lee.

When they came, Lee liked to eat.

Lee ate the tiny animals off the big fish.

This made the big fish happy.

And Lee got his lunch.   (62 words)

Unprompted Memories

Please retell the story.

_____ Lee the fish
_____ little, blue
_____ friends are big fish
_____ they lived far away
_____ swim to see Lee every day
_____ Lee ate little animals
_____ off big fish
_____ big fish happy
_____ Lee's lunch

Comprehension Questions

_____ *Who was Lee?*   (fish)
_____ *What did Lee look like?*   (little)
_____ (blue)
_____ *Who were Lee's friends?*   (big fish)
_____ *Where did his friends live?*   (far away)
_____ *When did his friends come to see Lee?*   (every day)
_____ *What did Lee do when they came?*   (ate little animals off the fish)
_____ *How did the big fish feel after Lee's meal?*   (happy)
_____ *Why did Lee like their visits?*   (got his lunch)

Interpretive question: *Why did the big fish feel happy after Lee ate the little animals off them?*

Acceptable answer: _____ Yes _____ No

Memories: _____ Unprompted + _____ Prompted = _____ Total

Organized retelling: _____ Yes _____ No

Oral reading inaccuracies changed meaning: _____ Yes _____ No

Rate appropriate: _____ Yes _____ No   Fluency appropriate: _____ Yes _____ No

_____ reads word by word   _____ reads in phrases   _____ good use of punctuation
_____ good use of stress, pitch, and intonation

Oral reading:

_____ Substitutions   _____ Mispronunciations
_____ Additions   _____ Repetitions
_____ Omissions   _____ Words pronounced by examiner

INSTRUCTIONAL LEVEL GUIDE   Prepared: 3 or fewer errors   Unprepared: 6 or fewer errors   6 or more memories

GRADED PASSAGE (PC/A)

Assessing and Activating Background Knowledge

Here is a story about turtles. What do you know about turtles?

_____ Adequate   _____ Inadequate

Motivating Statement   *Read the story to learn about turtles and why they are always at home.*

TURTLES AT HOME

Turtles are always at home.

If they visit the sea, they are at home.

If they go to the high hills, they are at home.

If they go far away, they have a home.

Turtles carry their homes with them.

Their shell is their house.

Turtles stay in their shells.

That is why they are always at home.   (58 words)

Unprompted Memories

Please retell the story.

_____ turtles at home

_____ visit sea, at home

_____ go to hills, at home

_____ go far away, have a home

_____ carry their home

_____ shell is a house

_____ stay in their shell

_____ why always home

Comprehension Questions

_____ *When are turtles at home?*   (always at home)

_____ *Where do turtles visit?*   (high hills)

_____ (sea)

_____ (far away)

_____ *What do the turtles carry all the time?*   (own home)

_____ *Where is the turtle's house?*   (on his back—his shell)

_____ *Why are the turtles always at home?*   (because they stay in their shells)

Interpretive question: *Why don't turtles leave their shells?*

        Acceptable answer: _____ Yes _____ No

Memories: _____ Unprompted + _____ Prompted = _____ Total

Organized retelling: _____ Yes _____ No

Oral reading inaccuracies changed meaning: _____ Yes _____ No

Rate appropriate: _____ Yes _____ No   Fluency appropriate: _____ Yes _____ No

        _____ reads word by word   _____ reads in phrases   _____ good use of punctuation

        _____ good use of stress, pitch, and intonation

Oral reading:

        _____ Substitutions   _____ Mispronunciations

        _____ Additions   _____ Repetitions

        _____ Omissions   _____ Words pronounced by examiner

INSTRUCTIONAL LEVEL GUIDE   Prepared: 3 or fewer errors   Unprepared: 6 or fewer errors   5 or more memories

GRADED PASSAGE (PA)

Assessing and Activating Background Knowledge

Here is a story about a slippery sidewalk. What problems can be caused by a slippery sidewalk?

_____ Adequate   _____ Inadequate

Motivating Statement   *Read the story to learn about the problems caused by this slippery sidewalk and what was done about it.*

A SLIPPERY SIDEWALK

It was a cold day.

A man fell on the ice.

He was not hurt.

"Put salt on the ice," said Bill.

"Salt will melt the ice."

"Salt can kill the grass," said Pat.

"Put sand on the ice."

"I will try to find some sand," said Bill.

"But it is better to kill some grass than

have a bad fall."   (61 words)

Unprompted Memories

Please retell the story.

_____ cold day

_____ man fell on ice, not hurt

_____ put salt on ice (Bill)

_____ salt kills grass (Pat)

_____ put sand on ice (Pat)

_____ will find some sand (Bill)

_____ better to kill grass than to have a bad fall

Comprehension Questions

_____ *What kind of day was it?*   (cold)

_____ *What happened to the man?*   (fell on ice)

_____ *How was the man after the fall?*   (not hurt)

_____ *What did Bill suggest?*   (put salt on ice)

_____ *Why did Bill suggest salt?*   (to melt ice)

_____ *Why did Pat say not to use salt?*   (kills grass)

_____ *What did Pat want to use?*   (sand)

_____ *What did Bill decide?*   (to find sand)

Interpretive question: *Why was Bill more concerned about people falling on the ice than about killing the grass?*

Acceptable answer: _____ Yes _____ No

Memories: _____ Unprompted + _____ Prompted = _____ Total

Organized retelling: _____ Yes _____ No

Oral reading inaccuracies changed meaning: _____ Yes _____ No

Rate appropriate: _____ Yes _____ No   Fluency appropriate: _____ Yes _____ No

_____ reads word by word   _____ reads in phrases   _____ good use of punctuation

_____ good use of stress, pitch, and intonation

Oral reading:

_____ Substitutions   _____ Mispronunciations

_____ Additions   _____ Repetitions

_____ Omissions   _____ Words pronounced by examiner

INSTRUCTIONAL LEVEL GUIDE   Prepared: 3 or fewer errors   Unprepared: 6 or fewer errors   5 or more memories

GRADED PASSAGE (1C)

Assessing and Activating Background Knowledge

Here is a story about a kitten and a girl named Pat. What is it like to have a kitten?

_____ Adequate   _____ Inadequate

Motivating Statement   *Read the story to learn about the girl named Pat and the kitten.*

PAT AND THE KITTEN

Pat saw a kitten. It was on the side of the street. It was sitting under a blue car.

"Come here, little kitten," Pat said. The kitten looked up at Pat. It had big yellow eyes. Pat took her from under the car. She saw that her leg was hurt.

"I will take care of you," Pat said. She put her hand on the kitten's soft, black fur. "You can come home with me."

The kitten gave a happy *meow*.   (80 words)

Unprompted Memories

Please retell the story.

_____ Pat saw kitten

_____ on side of street/under car

_____ come here, Pat said

_____ kitten looked up

_____ big yellow eyes, black fur

_____ her leg was hurt

_____ I will take care of you

_____ Pat put hand on fur

_____ come home with me

_____ kitten meowed happily

Comprehension Questions

_____ *What did Pat see?*   (kitten)

_____ *Where was the kitten?*   (side of street)

_____ (under car)

_____ *What did Pat first say to the kitten?*   (come here little kitten)

_____ *What did the kitten look like?*   (yellow eyes)

_____ (black fur)

_____ *What was the matter with the kitten?*   (hurt leg)

_____ *What did Pat say to the kitten when she saw it was hurt?*   (I will take care of you)

_____ *What did Pat want to do with the kitten?*   (take home)

_____ *What did the kitten do?*   (meowed happily)

Interpretive question: *Why was the kitten happy at the end of the story?*

        Acceptable answer: _____ Yes   _____ No

Memories: _____ Unprompted + _____ Prompted = _____ Total

Organized retelling: _____ Yes   _____ No

Oral reading inaccuracies changed meaning: _____ Yes   _____ No

Rate appropriate: _____ Yes   _____ No   Fluency appropriate: _____ Yes   _____ No

        _____ reads word by word   _____ reads in phrases   _____ good use of punctuation

        _____ good use of stress, pitch, and intonation

Oral reading:

        _____ Substitutions   _____ Mispronunciations

        _____ Additions   _____ Repetitions

        _____ Omissions   _____ Words pronounced by examiner

INSTRUCTIONAL LEVEL GUIDE   Prepared: 4 or fewer errors   Unprepared: 8 or fewer errors   6 or more memories

GRADED PASSAGE (1C/A)

Assessing and Activating Background Knowledge

Here is a story about a man named Tony who lived in a city. What do you think he didn't like about the city?

_____ Adequate   _____ Inadequate

Motivating Statement   *Read the story to learn about Tony and what he did in the city.*

TONY AND THE FLOWER SHOP

Tony lived in a big city. He ran a flower shop. Tony loved his flowers, for the flowers did not make any noise. Tony loved peace and quiet.

The city where Tony lived was noisy. The buses, trucks, and cars were very noisy. He did not like the noise of the city.

Without the quiet Tony found in the flower shop, he would have moved from the city. The flower shop was his only reason for staying in the city.   (80 words)

Unprompted Memories

Please retell the story.

_____ Tony lived in a city

_____ ran a flower shop

_____ loved his flowers, quiet

_____ city was noisy

_____ buses, trucks, cars

_____ without quiet of shop

_____ he would move from city

_____ flower shop was

_____ reason for staying in city

Comprehension Questions

_____ *Where did Tony live?*   (big city)

_____ *What did Tony do?*   (ran flower shop)

_____ *Why did Tony like his flowers?*   (they were quiet)

_____ *Why did Tony dislike the city?*   (the noise)

_____ *Why was the city noisy?*   (buses)

_____ (trucks)

_____ (cars)

_____ *What did the flower shop give Tony?*   (peace and quiet)

_____ *What was the reason for staying in the city?*   (he liked his flower shop)

Interpretive question: *Why do you think Tony likes peace and quiet?*

    Acceptable answer: _____ Yes _____ No

Memories: _____ Unprompted + _____ Prompted = _____ Total

Organized retelling: _____ Yes _____ No

Oral reading inaccuracies changed meaning: _____ Yes _____ No

Rate appropriate: _____ Yes _____ No   Fluency appropriate: _____ Yes _____ No

    _____ reads word by word   _____ reads in phrases   _____ good use of punctuation

    _____ good use of stress, pitch, and intonation

Oral reading:

    _____ Substitutions   _____ Mispronunciations

    _____ Additions   _____ Repetitions

    _____ Omissions   _____ Words pronounced by examiner

INSTRUCTIONAL LEVEL GUIDE   Prepared: 4 or fewer errors   Unprepared: 8 or fewer errors   6 or more memories

GRADED PASSAGE (1A)

Assessing and Activating Background Knowledge

Here is a story about an old man who solved a problem. What kinds of problems do elderly people have?

_____ Adequate   _____ Inadequate

Motivating Statement   *Read the story to learn about some things an old man did and how he made his life easier.*

GIVE ME ROOM

I saw an old man get on the bus. He walked very slowly. He used a cane. I looked at the cane with surprise. The man had a bike horn on it. I told him I had never seen a cane with a horn. "Have you ever been to the city market?" he asked. I said that I had. "Then you know it is crowded," he said. "People did not give me room. Now I honk my horn and they move."   (81 words)

Unprompted Memories

Please retell the story.

_____ saw old man on bus
_____ walked slowly using cane
_____ surprised at horn on cane
_____ never saw a cane with horn
_____ been to market? he asked
_____ said yes
_____ it is crowded, he said
_____ people didn't give me room
_____ now honks and they move

Comprehension Questions

_____ *Who did the person see?*   (an old man)
_____ *What was the old man doing?*   (riding a bus)
_____ *Describe the old man.*   (walked slow)
_____ (used a cane)
_____ *Why was the person surprised?*   (had horn on a cane)
_____ *What did the person say to the old man?*   (never saw cane with horn on it)
_____ *What caused the problem for the old man?*   (crowded market)
_____ *Why did the person understand the problem at the market?* (he had been there)
_____ *Why did he use a horn?*   (to get people to move)

Interpretive question: *Why did people move when he honked?*

    Acceptable answer: _____ Yes _____ No

Memories: _____ Unprompted + _____ Prompted = _____ Total

Organized retelling: _____ Yes _____ No

Oral reading inaccuracies changed meaning: _____ Yes _____ No

Rate appropriate: _____ Yes _____ No   Fluency appropriate: _____ Yes _____ No

    _____ reads word by word   _____ reads in phrases   _____ good use of punctuation

    _____ good use of stress, pitch, and intonation

Oral reading:

    _____ Substitutions   _____ Mispronunciations

    _____ Additions   _____ Repetitions

    _____ Omissions   _____ Words pronounced by examiner

INSTRUCTIONAL LEVEL GUIDE   Prepared: 4 or fewer errors   Unprepared: 8 or fewer errors   6 or more memories

GRADED PASSAGE (2C)

Assessing and Activating Background Knowledge

Here is a story about a little frog. What do you know about frogs?

_____ Adequate   _____ Inadequate

Motivating Statement   *Read the story to learn how this little frog lived.*

THE SONG OF LITTLE FROG

Little Frog lived by a lake. He did not have many things. He only had a house to live in, a bed to sleep in, and an old pot to cook with. He had one old book that he read again and again. Still Little Frog was happy.

Near his house there were many pretty flowers. The birds sang all day. Little Frog liked to look at the pretty flowers. He liked to hear the birds sing. Little Frog wanted to sing like the birds. But when he tried to sing, all that came out was a *ribbit ribbit.*   (99 words)

Unprompted Memories	Comprehension Questions
Please retell the story.	_____ *Where did Little Frog live?* (by a lake)
_____ Little Frog	_____ (in a house)
_____ lived by a lake	_____ *What did he own?* (pot)
_____ had a house, bed, and pot	_____ (bed)
_____ had an old book	_____ *Why did he read the same book?* (only had one book)
_____ read again and again	_____ *How did Little Frog feel?* (happy)
_____ near house flowers, birds	_____ *What things were near his house?* (flowers)
_____ he wanted to	_____ (birds)
_____ sing like birds	_____ *Why did he like the birds?* (they sang)
_____ when he tried	_____ *What happened when he tried to sing?* (ribbit ribbit)
_____ just *ribbit ribbit*	

Interpretive question: *Why was Little Frog happy with just a few things?*

        Acceptable answer: _____ Yes   _____ No

Memories: _____ Unprompted + _____ Prompted = _____ Total

Organized retelling: _____ Yes   _____ No

Oral reading inaccuracies changed meaning: _____ Yes   _____ No

Rate appropriate: _____ Yes   _____ No   Fluency appropriate: _____ Yes   _____ No

        _____ reads word by word   _____ reads in phrases   _____ good use of punctuation

        _____ good use of stress, pitch, and intonation

Oral reading:

        _____ Substitutions   _____ Mispronunciations

        _____ Additions   _____ Repetitions

        _____ Omissions   _____ Words pronounced by examiner

INSTRUCTIONAL LEVEL GUIDE   Prepared: 5 or fewer errors   Unprepared: 10 or fewer errors   6 or more memories

GRADED PASSAGE (2C/A)

Assessing and Activating Background Knowledge

Here is a story about an unusual newspaper. Why do most people read newspapers?

_____ Adequate   _____ Inadequate

Motivating Statement   *Read the story to learn how a boy helps someone.*

SAM BUYS A NEWSPAPER

Sam stopped to ask Mrs. Kay if she needed anything from the store. She was very old. Sam liked to help her. She asked him to buy her a newspaper.

The store was closed. Sam walked for a long time to another store. He asked for a newspaper. One was folded and put into his bag.

Sam gave Mrs. Kay the paper. She said, "Oh, Sam, you are so good. I have not seen a paper written in Greek for months!"

Sam was surprised, but he just said, "You're welcome, Mrs. Kay."   (92 words)

Unprompted Memories	**Comprehension Questions**
Please retell the story.	_____ *Where did Sam go?* (store or Mrs. Kay's)
_____ Sam going to store	_____ *What did Sam ask Mrs. Kay?* (if she needed anything)
_____ he stopped at Mrs. Kay's	_____ *Why did Sam stop at Mrs. Kay's?* (he wanted to help)
_____ if she needed anything	_____ *Why did he like to help Mrs. Kay?* (she's old or she needed help)
_____ Mrs. Kay is old; Sam likes to help	_____ *What did Mrs. Kay need at the store?* (a newspaper)
_____ she needed a paper	_____ *Why did Sam walk a long way?* (store was closed)
_____ store was closed	_____ *Where did he finally get what he needed?* (another store)
_____ walked a long way	_____ *What did Sam buy at the store?* (newspaper)
_____ to another store	_____ *What did Mrs. Kay say?* (she hadn't seen a Greek newspaper or
_____ paper folded and put into bag	Sam was good)
_____ gave paper to Mrs. Kay	_____ *What did Sam say to Mrs. Kay?* (you're welcome)
_____ she said Sam was good	
_____ she hadn't seen Greek paper in long time	
_____ Sam surprised, said you're welcome	

Interpretive question: *Why did Sam get a Greek newspaper at that particular store?*

    Acceptable answer: _____ Yes _____ No

Memories: _____ Unprompted + _____ Prompted = _____ Total

Organized retelling: _____ Yes _____ No

Oral reading inaccuracies changed meaning: _____ Yes _____ No

Rate appropriate: _____ Yes _____ No   Fluency appropriate: _____ Yes _____ No

        _____ reads word by word   _____ reads in phrases   _____ good use of punctuation

        _____ good use of stress, pitch, and intonation

Oral reading:

    _____ Substitutions   _____ Mispronunciations

    _____ Additions   _____ Repetitions

    _____ Omissions   _____ Words pronounced by examiner

INSTRUCTIONAL LEVEL GUIDE   Prepared: 5 or fewer errors   Unprepared: 9 or fewer errors   6 or more memories

GRADED PASSAGE (2A)

Assessing and Activating Background Knowledge
Here is a story about Linda, who works in a diner. What is a diner?

_____ Adequate   _____ Inadequate

Motivating Statement   *Read the story to learn what Linda does to improve or make her life better.*

LINDA AT THE DINER

Linda has a part-time job in a diner. She works in the morning from six until ten. The diner is busy at breakfast time. Linda works hard, but she likes her job at the diner. She likes talking with people. Many of the same people come in every day.

At night Linda goes to school. She likes night school. She has made new friends in her classes. The teachers are very nice.

Linda wants to learn more about business. She hopes to become a manager of a diner. Then she wants to buy her own diner someday.   (97 words)

Unprompted Memories

Please retell the story.
- _____ Linda has part-time job
- _____ at diner from 6 A.M. until 10 A.M.
- _____ diner busy at breakfast
- _____ likes talking to people
- _____ goes to night school
- _____ likes night school
- _____ made new friends
- _____ teachers nice
- _____ to study business
- _____ hopes to become manager
- _____ wants to buy own diner

Comprehension Questions
- _____ *Where does Linda work?*   (at diner)
- _____ *When does Linda work?*   (6–10)
- _____ *When is the diner busy?*   (breakfast time)
- _____ *Why does Linda like to work at the diner?*   (talk with people)
- _____ *What does Linda do in the evening?*   (goes to night school)
- _____ (new friends)
- _____ *Why does Linda go to school?*   (learn business)
- _____ *What does she want to do someday?*   (manage diner)
- _____ (buy her own)

Interpretive question: *Why does Linda feel she should go to night school?*

Acceptable answer: _____ Yes   _____ No

Memories: _____ Unprompted + _____ Prompted = _____ Total

Organized retelling: _____ Yes   _____ No

Oral reading inaccuracies changed meaning: _____ Yes   _____ No

Rate appropriate: _____ Yes   _____ No   Fluency appropriate: _____ Yes   _____ No

_____ reads word by word   _____ reads in phrases   _____ good use of punctuation

_____ good use of stress, pitch, and intonation

Oral reading:
- _____ Substitutions   _____ Mispronunciations
- _____ Additions   _____ Repetitions
- _____ Omissions   _____ Words pronounced by examiner

INSTRUCTIONAL LEVEL GUIDE   Prepared: 5 or fewer errors   Unprepared: 10 or fewer errors   6 or more memories

GRADED PASSAGE (3C)

Assessing and Activating Background Knowledge

Here is a story about a boy named James and how he hurt himself. What is it like to have an accident and hurt yourself?

_____ Adequate   _____ Inadequate

Motivating Statement   *Read the story to learn about the accident that James had and what was done to help him.*

JAMES' CUT

It was after lunch when James cut his finger on the playground. He was bleeding and he hurt a little, too.

He went inside to find his teacher. He showed her his cut finger and asked for a Band-Aid. She looked at it and said, "Well, it's not too bad, James. I think we should wash it before we bandage it, don't you?" James did not want it washed because he thought it would sting. But he was afraid to tell Miss Smith. He just acted brave.

When it was washed and bandaged, he thanked Miss Smith. Then he rushed out to the playground to show everyone his shiny new bandage.   (111 words)

Unprompted Memories

Please retell the story.

_____ James cut finger
_____ on playground after lunch
_____ bleeding and hurt
_____ went to teacher, showed finger
_____ asked for a Band-Aid
_____ she looked and said wash first
_____ then bandage
_____ James didn't want it washed
_____ he thought it would sting
_____ acted brave when washed and bandaged
_____ said thank you, went back to playground
_____ showed his new bandage

Comprehension Questions

_____ *What happened to James?*   (cut his finger)
_____ *When did he hurt himself?*   (after lunch)
_____ *Where did the accident happen?*   (on the playground)
_____ *Where did James go when he cut his finger?*   (inside school to find teacher)
_____ *What did the teacher say?*   (they should wash it)
_____ *Why didn't James want it washed?*   (thought it would sting)
_____ *How did James act when his finger was washed?*   (brave)
_____ *What did he do after it was bandaged?*   (said thank you)
_____ (went back to playground)
_____ *What did he show his friends?*   (new bandage)

Interpretive question: *Why didn't James want to tell Miss Smith he was afraid to have his finger washed?*
         Acceptable answer: _____ Yes _____ No
Memories: _____ Unprompted + _____ Prompted = _____ Total
Organized retelling: _____ Yes _____ No
Oral reading inaccuracies changed meaning: _____ Yes _____ No
Rate appropriate: _____ Yes _____ No   Fluency appropriate: _____ Yes _____ No
         _____ reads word by word   _____ reads in phrases   _____ good use of punctuation
         _____ good use of stress, pitch, and intonation
Oral reading:
         _____ Substitutions   _____ Mispronunciations
         _____ Additions   _____ Repetitions
         _____ Omissions   _____ Words pronounced by examiner

INSTRUCTIONAL LEVEL GUIDE   Prepared: 6 or fewer errors   Unprepared: 11 or fewer errors   6 or more memories

GRADED PASSAGE (3C/A)

Assessing and Activating Background Knowledge

Here is a story about astronauts and deep-sea divers. What do they have in common?

_____ Adequate   _____ Inadequate

Motivating Statement   *Read the story to learn about what astronauts and deep-sea divers do.*

TODAY'S EXPLORERS

Astronauts fly far away from the earth. They explore space and the moon. Maybe, in time, they will explore other worlds, too. Deep-sea divers go to the floor of the sea. They explore places just as strange and wonderful as astronauts do.

You may have seen some beautiful fish in the ocean. If you were a diver, you could go far under water. You could stay there long enough to see many unusual creatures. You would find things you never dreamed of.

The only way you could stay under water for more than a short time is to use special gear. You must use the same kind of gear divers use. A large air tank lets you stay under water for an hour.

Today, explorers go under the sea and far into space.   (133 words)

Unprompted Memories

Please retell the story.

_____ astronauts fly from earth

_____ explore moon and space, other worlds

_____ deep-sea divers go to sea floor

_____ they explore strange and wonderful places

_____ may have seen fish in ocean

_____ divers go far under water

_____ may see unusual creatures

_____ find things you never dream of

_____ stay under, use special gear

_____ kind of gear divers use

_____ air tank lets you stay under water for an hour

_____ explorers go under sea and into space

Comprehension Questions

_____ *Where do astronauts explore?*   (space and moon)

_____ *Where might they explore in future?*   (other worlds)

_____ *Where do divers explore?*   (sea floor)

_____ *What may you have seen in the ocean?*   (beautiful fish)

_____ *What could you see if you were a diver?*   (unusual creatures or things you haven't dreamed of)

_____ *How do divers stay under water?*   (use special gear or air tank)

_____ *How long can a larger air tank let you stay under water?*   (an hour)

_____ *Where do explorers go today?*   (under sea and into space)

Interpretive question: *Why do astronauts and deep-sea divers enjoy their jobs?*

Acceptable answer: _____ Yes   _____ No

Memories: _____ Unprompted + _____ Prompted = _____ Total

Organized retelling: _____ Yes   _____ No

Oral reading inaccuracies changed meaning: _____ Yes   _____ No

Rate appropriate: _____ Yes   _____ No   Fluency appropriate: _____ Yes   _____ No

_____ reads word by word   _____ reads in phrases   _____ good use of punctuation

_____ good use of stress, pitch, and intonation

Oral reading:

_____ Substitutions   _____ Mispronunciations

_____ Additions   _____ Repetitions

_____ Omissions   _____ Words pronounced by examiner

INSTRUCTIONAL LEVEL GUIDE   Prepared: 7 or fewer errors   Unprepared: 13 or fewer errors   5 or more memories

GRADED PASSAGE (3A)

Assessing and Activating Background Knowledge

Here is a story about a lucky wrong number. What usually happens if you dial the wrong number on the telephone?

_____ Adequate   _____ Inadequate

Motivating Statement   *Read the story to learn what happened as a result of a wrong number.*

THE LUCKY WRONG NUMBER

Sue and Bill were eating dinner when the telephone rang. Bill said, "I'll get it." A man asked if the washer could be delivered in the morning.

Bill said, "We did not order a washer."

The man said, "Is this the home of P. J. Johnson?"

"No," Bill said, "but wait; P. J. Johnson is our uncle's name, and we haven't seen him in a long time. What address do you have for him?"

The caller said, "201 Second Street."

Bill and Sue went to the address of P. J. Johnson. He was their uncle. They were happy to see each other. Later Sue said, "Buying that washer was lucky."

Uncle P. J. laughed, "I didn't buy a washer; I bought a TV. We just had a lucky wrong number."   (126 words)

Unprompted Memories

Please retell the story.

_____ Bill and Sue eating dinner
_____ phone rang
_____ asked about delivering washer
_____ we did not buy washer
_____ is this P. J. Johnson's home
_____ no, but that is uncle's name
_____ haven't seen him for long time
_____ asked for address and went there
_____ he was uncle; glad to see one another
_____ buying washer good luck
_____ didn't buy washer, bought TV
_____ lucky wrong number

Comprehension Questions

_____ *What were Bill and Sue doing at the beginning of the story?* (eating dinner)
_____ *What happened while they were eating?*   (phone rang)
_____ *What did the caller want?*   (see if washer could be delivered)
_____ *Why was this a confusing situation?*   (they didn't order a new washer)
_____ *Where was the washer supposed to go?*   (P. J. Johnson)
_____ *Who was P. J. Johnson?*   (their uncle)
_____ *What did Bill and Sue ask the caller for?*   (the address of P. J. Johnson)
_____ *Where did Bill and Sue go then?*   (P. J. Johnson's address)
_____ *Why were they happy to see one another?*   (hadn't seen each other in long time)
_____ *What did their uncle buy?*   (TV)

Interpretive question: *How did the situation in the story help get relatives together?*
      Acceptable answer: _____ Yes   _____ No
Memories: _____ Unprompted + _____ Prompted = _____ Total
Organized retelling: _____ Yes   _____ No
Oral reading inaccuracies changed meaning: _____ Yes   _____ No
Rate appropriate: _____ Yes   _____ No   Fluency appropriate: _____ Yes   _____ No
      _____ reads word by word   _____ reads in phrases   _____ good use of punctuation
      _____ good use of stress, pitch, and intonation
Oral reading:
      _____ Substitutions   _____ Mispronunciations
      _____ Additions   _____ Repetitions
      _____ Omissions   _____ Words pronounced by examiner

INSTRUCTIONAL LEVEL GUIDE   Prepared: 6 or fewer errors   Unprepared: 13 or fewer errors   6 or more memories

GRADED PASSAGE (4C)

Assessing and Activating Background Knowledge

Here is a story about a handicapped little girl. What does it mean to have a disability?

_____ Adequate   _____ Inadequate

Motivating Statement   *Read the story to learn about the disability the little girl has and some things she does to help herself.*

CHECKERS GAME FOR KIM

Kim has an arm that does not work well. Sometimes Kim gets angry with her left arm because it doesn't do what she wants it to and accidents happen. When this happens, Kim gets mad and she calls her arm useless. Kim knows that with lots of exercise her left arm will work better and she will be able to do more things. Kim tries to exercise her arm as much as she can. Exercise is very hard work, but Kim keeps trying.

One way that Kim likes to exercise her arm is to help her dad make things in the workshop. She has fun working with her dad. They have just finished making a special checkers game. The checkers go into holes in the board. This will help Kim. The holes will keep the checkers from being knocked off the board by her arm. She enjoyed helping make the game because she loves to play checkers. Kim likes to work with her dad, and it is good exercise for her arm.   (171 words)

Unprompted Memories

Please retell the story.

_____ Kim's arm doesn't work well
_____ she gets angry
_____ because it doesn't work the way she wants
_____ Kim calls her arm useless
_____ exercise will make it better
_____ exercise is very hard, but she keeps trying
_____ one way to exercise is to help her dad in shop
_____ she has fun working with her dad
_____ they finished checkers game
_____ checkers go into holes
_____ keep from being knocked off by arm
_____ she enjoyed helping make game
_____ loves to play checkers
_____ good exercise for arm, too

Comprehension Questions

_____ *What was the matter with Kim?* (she was disabled, had a bad arm)
_____ *What could Kim do to help her arm?* (exercise)
_____ *What was Kim's attitude about exercise?* (she knew it was hard, but kept trying)
_____ *What will lots of exercise do for Kim's arm?* (make it better)
_____ *What was one way she exercised?* (worked with her dad in workshop)
_____ *What did they just finish making?* (a special checkers game)
_____ *How was the board made?* (holes for checkers)
_____ *Why was the new board good for Kim?* (she couldn't knock checkers off board)

Interpretive question: *Why do you think that Kim got angry and called her arm useless?*
      Acceptable answer: _____ Yes   _____ No
Memories: _____ Unprompted + _____ Prompted = _____ Total
Organized retelling: _____ Yes   _____ No
Oral reading inaccuracies changed meaning: _____ Yes   _____ No
Rate appropriate: _____ Yes   _____ No   Fluency appropriate: _____ Yes   _____ No
      _____ reads word by word   _____ reads in phrases   _____ good use of punctuation
      _____ good use of stress, pitch, and intonation
Oral reading:
      _____ Substitutions   _____ Mispronunciations
      _____ Additions   _____ Repetitions
      _____ Omissions   _____ Words pronounced by examiner

INSTRUCTIONAL LEVEL GUIDE   Prepared: 3 or fewer errors   Unprepared: 9 or fewer errors   5 or more memories

GRADED PASSAGE (4C/A)

Assessing and Activating Background Knowledge

Here is a story about a little girl who was sick for a long time. How do you feel if you are sick?

_____ Adequate   _____ Inadequate

Motivating Statement   *Read the story to learn how the lives of the girl and her mother change.*

THE RECOVERY

In three small rooms lived a mother and her daughter, who was quite ill. The mother worked every day. She worked hard but could afford little more than rent, food, and clothes. Because of this, the little sick girl would stay quietly in bed at home while her mother was away.

The mother worried about her daughter. If only she had someone to talk to or something to keep her mind busy.

One morning as the mother was leaving for work, she saw a little hurt bird huddled on the window sill. Her daughter insisted that it be brought in so she could care for it.

That evening when the mother returned, the daughter was more talkative than she had been for a while. Every evening after that, she noticed that both the girl and the bird were improved. They seemed to draw strength from each other.

Then one day the mother returned home to find the table set. Tears came to the mother's eyes when the little girl said they must celebrate, for the bird was better.   (178 words)

Unprompted Memories

Please retell the story.

_____ three small rooms
_____ lived a mother and sick girl
_____ mother worked hard every day
_____ she could afford only food, rent, and clothes
_____ mother worried about daughter
_____ needed someone to talk to
_____ keep her mind busy
_____ saw hurt bird on sill
_____ brought it in for girl to care for
_____ girl more talkative
_____ when mother came home
_____ both bird and girl improved

Comprehension Questions

_____ *Where did the mother and daughter live?*   (in three small rooms)
_____ *What was the matter with the little girl?*   (she was sick)
_____ *What did the mother do every day?*   (worked hard)
_____ *What could the mother afford?*   (food, rent, clothes—2 of 3)
_____ *What was found on the window sill?*   (a little hurt bird)
_____ *What was done with the bird?*   (brought in for girl to care for)
_____ *How was the girl different when the mother came home?*   (more talkative)
_____ *What did the mother find when she came home?*   (table was set)
_____ *What did they celebrate?*   (the bird's recovery)

Interpretive question: *How did taking care of the bird help the girl?*

        Acceptable answer: _____ Yes   _____ No
Memories: _____ Unprompted + _____ Prompted = _____ Total
Organized retelling: _____ Yes   _____ No
Oral reading inaccuracies changed meaning: _____ Yes   _____ No
Rate appropriate: _____ Yes   _____ No   Fluency appropriate: _____ Yes   _____ No
        _____ reads word by word   _____ reads in phrases   _____ good use of punctuation
        _____ good use of stress, pitch, and intonation
Oral reading:
        _____ Substitutions   _____ Mispronunciations
        _____ Additions   _____ Repetitions
        _____ Omissions   _____ Words pronounced by examiner

INSTRUCTIONAL LEVEL GUIDE   Prepared: 4 or fewer errors   Unprepared: 9 or fewer errors   6 or more memories

GRADED PASSAGE (4A)

Assessing and Activating Background Knowledge

Here is a story about Alaska. What do you know about Alaska?

_____ Adequate   _____ Inadequate

Motivating Statement   *Read the story to learn about the purchase of Alaska and what that state is like.*

LAND OF MANY RICHES

In 1869, the American Secretary of State, William Seward, did something that many people thought was foolish. He bought a huge piece of land called Alaska. He bought Alaska for only two cents an acre from a country called Russia. But many people thought the purchase was a waste of money. To them, Alaska was just a useless land of rocks, snow, and ice.

However, the following years have proved these people wrong. Some of the riches found in Alaska have made the purchase worthwhile. One of these riches is the trees in Alaska's huge forests. Much of the land in Alaska is covered by forests. The trees are cut and sold to all parts of the world.

The sea around Alaska is full of riches, too. Many fish, such as codfish, herring, crabs, and shrimp, live there. They are caught and sold to the rest of the United States and the world. Alaska has been worth much more than it cost because many riches have been discovered there.   (169 words)

Unprompted Memories

Please retell the story.

_____ in 1869 Secretary of State Seward
_____ did something people thought was foolish
_____ bought the land called Alaska
_____ for two cents an acre from Russia
_____ people thought it was a waste of money
_____ Alaska useless land of ice, snow, and rock
_____ time proved them wrong
_____ riches proved worthwhile
_____ among riches are trees
_____ trees cover land
_____ they are cut and sold around the world
_____ surrounding sea full of riches
_____ among these are codfish, herring, crabs, and shrimp
_____ caught and sold all over world
_____ Alaska worth more than its cost because of its riches

Comprehension Questions

_____ *Who purchased Alaska?*   (Sec. of State Seward)
_____ *In what year was the purchase made?*   (1869)
_____ *What did some people think of the purchase?* (very foolish)
_____ *How much did Alaska cost?*   (two cents an acre)
_____ *From what country was Alaska purchased?* (Russia)
_____ *Why did people say Alaska was useless?* (covered with snow, rocks, and ice)
_____ *What do they do with the trees?*   (cut and sell all over United States and world)
_____ *What riches are found in the sea?*   (fish)
_____ *What do they do with the fish?*   (sell them all over the world)
_____ *Why was Alaska worth more than its price?* (all the riches)

Interpretive question: *Why is it important for a country to have different kinds of riches?*
        Acceptable answer: _____ Yes   _____ No
Memories: _____ Unprompted + _____ Prompted = _____ Total
Organized retelling: _____ Yes   _____ No
Oral reading inaccuracies changed meaning: _____ Yes   _____ No
Rate appropriate: _____ Yes   _____ No   Fluency appropriate: _____ Yes   _____ No
        _____ reads word by word   _____ reads in phrases   _____ good use of punctuation
        _____ good use of stress, pitch, and intonation
Oral reading:
        _____ Substitutions   _____ Mispronunciations
        _____ Additions   _____ Repetitions
        _____ Omissions   _____ Words pronounced by examiner

INSTRUCTIONAL LEVEL GUIDE   Prepared: 3 or fewer errors   Unprepared: 8 or fewer errors   6 or more memories

GRADED PASSAGE (5C)

Assessing and Activating Background Knowledge

Here is a story about a young hunter and an eagle. What do you know about eagles?

_____ Adequate   _____ Inadequate

Motivating Statement   *Read the story to learn about the hunting adventure the boy had.*

WAUKEWA'S EAGLE

One morning when the boy called Waukewa was hunting along the mountainside, he found a young eagle with a broken wing. It was lying at the base of a cliff. The bird had fallen from a ledge and, being too young to fly, had fluttered down the cliff. It was hurt so severely that it was likely to die. When Waukewa saw it, he was about to drive one of his sharp arrows through its body. But then he saw that the young eagle at his feet was quivering with pain and fright. Waukewa slowly stooped over the panting eagle. The wild eyes of the wounded bird and the keen, dark eyes of the boy met. The boy's eyes grew gentler and softer as he gazed at the bird. Then the struggling of the young eagle stopped. The wild, frightened look passed out of its eyes. And the bird allowed Waukewa to pass his hand gently over its ruffled feathers. The desire to fight, to defend its life, gave way to the charm of the tenderness and pity expressed in the boy's eyes. From that moment, Waukewa and the eagle were friends.   (192 words)

Comprehension Questions

_____ *Who was Waukewa?*   (a boy)
_____ *Where did he find the eagle?*   (at the base of a cliff)
_____ *What injury did the eagle have when Waukewa found it?*   (broken wing)
_____ *How was the eagle's wing broken?*   (in a fall)
_____ *What was Waukewa going to do to the eagle when he first saw it?*   (kill it—put an arrow through its body)
_____ *What made Waukewa change his mind about killing the bird?*   (he decided he wanted to keep the bird himself)
_____ *Why did the eagle decide not to fight and defend his life?*   (it realized that the boy was not going to hurt him)

Interpretive question: *Why do some wild animals or birds become friends with their enemy, humans?*
       Acceptable answer: _____ Yes _____ No
Memories: _____ Unprompted + _____ Prompted = _____ Total
Organized retelling: _____ Yes _____ No
Oral reading inaccuracies changed meaning: _____ Yes _____ No
Rate appropriate: _____ Yes _____ No   Fluency appropriate: _____ Yes _____ No
       _____ reads word by word   _____ reads in phrases   _____ good use of punctuation
       _____ good use of stress, pitch, and intonation
Oral reading:
       _____ Substitutions   _____ Mispronunciations
       _____ Additions   _____ Repetitions
       _____ Omissions   _____ Words pronounced by examiner

INSTRUCTIONAL LEVEL GUIDE   Prepared: 4 or fewer errors   Unprepared: 10 or fewer errors   5 or more memories

GRADED PASSAGE (5C/A)

Assessing and Activating Background Knowledge
Here is a story about the Nile Valley. Why would building a water system be helpful to grow crops?

_____ Adequate _____ Inadequate

Motivating Statement *Read the story to learn about what the tribes who settled in the Nile Valley did.*

THE NILE VALLEY

The early settlers in the Nile Valley had to root out the jungle and drain the marshes. Once it was cleared, the flood-enriched soil produced good crops. The rich soil caused many tribes to come to settle in the valley. In time some of these tribes learned that more land could be farmed if there was water for the long dry season. They worked hard to build a lake in which to store the water. They dug miles of canals and ditches to distribute the water to the fields.

This was a large task, which required the work of many tribes. Out of common need, the many different tribes had one leader to plan and direct their work. Once the water system was built, the leader supervised its repair and controlled the flow of water into the canals. Through his control of the water, he became a powerful ruler. (149 words)

Comprehension Questions
_____ *What did the early settlers of the Nile Valley have to do to the land?* (root out jungle and drain marshes)
_____ *Why did the soil produce good crops?* (flood-enriched)
_____ *Why did many tribes come to this region?* (the good soil produced good crops, so they could prosper there)
_____ *What did the tribes learn would help during the dry season?* (build something to store the water)
_____ *How was the water going to be distributed?* (through miles of ditches and canals)
_____ *Why did so many different tribes agree to one leader?* (they had a common need and all banded together to build the water system)
_____ *Why did this ruler become a powerful man?* (he controlled the water)

Interpretive question: *Why did the early settlers of the Nile Valley want to farm the land?*
Acceptable answer: _____ Yes _____ No
Memories: _____ Unprompted + _____ Prompted = _____ Total
Organized retelling: _____ Yes _____ No
Oral reading inaccuracies changed meaning: _____ Yes _____ No
Rate appropriate: _____ Yes _____ No   Fluency appropriate: _____ Yes _____ No
_____ reads word by word _____ reads in phrases _____ good use of punctuation
_____ good use of stress, pitch, and intonation
Oral reading:
_____ Substitutions _____ Mispronunciations
_____ Additions _____ Repetitions
_____ Omissions _____ Words pronounced by examiner

INSTRUCTIONAL LEVEL GUIDE Prepared: 3 or fewer errors Unprepared: 8 or fewer errors 5 or more memories

GRADED PASSAGE (5A)

Assessing and Activating Background Knowledge

Here is a story about a man who needs glasses. Why is it so important to wear glasses if needed?

_____ Adequate   _____ Inadequate

Motivating Statement   *Read the story to learn about what happened to Carlos and the effect of eyeglasses on reading.*

NOT IN THE MOOD TO READ

Have you ever heard someone say, "I used to like to read, but now I am not interested in reading"? Carlos used to say that. Then one day he found that he could not read the small print on a medicine bottle. Carlos had his eyes tested, and he was told he needed glasses. The day Carlos put them on, he stopped at a paperback book store and bought a sports magazine, a paperback mystery, and a newspaper. Carlos's eyes had never hurt, so he hadn't thought about needing glasses. It seemed good to be reading again. Carlos had forgotten how much he enjoyed reading.

There are many people, both children and adults, who believe they don't feel like reading or doing close work. Their vision is poor, but they do not know that they are having problems with their sight. However, there are others who know they should wear glasses but don't want to wear them. They think glasses may not be attractive. This is not necessarily true. Glasses now have such nice looking frames that some people wear them who don't need them! In fact, lenses in their glasses are just plain window glass.   (195 words)

Comprehension Questions

_____ *What do some people say about reading?*   (they used to like to read but don't read anymore)
_____ *What happened to Carlos one day?*   (he couldn't read the label on a medicine bottle)
_____ *After he got his glasses, what did Carlos buy?*   (a mystery, a sports magazine, and a newspaper)
_____ *Why did Carlos think that nothing was wrong with his eyes?*   (his eyes didn't hurt him)
_____ *Why do some people probably not like to read?*   (they have problems with their eyes)
_____ *Why do some people dislike glasses?*   (they think they are unattractive)
_____ *Why do some people have window glasses instead of lenses?*   (they like the looks of glasses but don't need to wear them)

Interpretive question: *Why is reading a hobby enjoyed by people with good eyesight?*
        Acceptable answer: _____ Yes _____ No
Memories: _____ Unprompted + _____ Prompted = _____ Total
Organized retelling: _____ Yes _____ No
Oral reading inaccuracies changed meaning: _____ Yes _____ No
Rate appropriate: _____ Yes _____ No   Fluency appropriate: _____ Yes _____ No
        _____ reads word by word   _____ reads in phrases   _____ good use of punctuation
        _____ good use of stress, pitch, and intonation
Oral reading:
        _____ Substitutions   _____ Mispronunciations
        _____ Additions   _____ Repetitions
        _____ Omissions   _____ Words pronounced by examiner

INSTRUCTIONAL LEVEL GUIDE   Prepared: 4 or fewer errors   Unprepared: 10 or fewer errors   5 or more memories

GRADED PASSAGE (6C)

Assessing and Activating Background Knowledge

Here is a story about primitive tools. What would primitive tools be like?

_____ Adequate   _____ Inadequate

Motivating Statement   *Read the story to learn about how primitive tools were made and used.*

EARLY TOOLS

Before humans discovered how to obtain and work metals, they made their tools out of wood, bone, and stone. At first they simply used the materials in their natural forms. Then they learned to alter the materials to produce tools to fit the tasks. Wood was split or shaved with sharp rocks and polished on sandstones. Pointed stones were used to bore holes in wood. Fire was also used to shape wood. After a portion of the wood was burnt, the charcoal was scraped away. This process was repeated until the desired shape was achieved.

Bone was broken into many different-sized splinters that were used as gouges, knives, and needles.

For the most part, the wood and bone tools have not survived to this day. But it is still possible to find ancient stone tools.

Stone tools were shaped by two methods. They were struck with rocks or pieces of antler or shaped by applying pressure at points where a flake was likely to break off.

Many people have found arrowheads. Most of these were actually used as spear points. Only a very small stone head would be light enough to use with an arrow and bow.   (197 words)

Comprehension Questions

_____ *What did humans use to make tools before metal was discovered?*   (wood, bone, and stone)
_____ *How did they use these materials?*   (first in natural form, then they learned to alter material)
_____ *How was wood altered to produce tools?*   (split or shaved, polished, and burned)
_____ *For what was bone used?*   (gouges, knives, and needles)
_____ *What two methods were used for shape stones?*   (struck with rock or antlers, pressure was applied where a flake was likely to break off)
_____ *What were arrowheads actually used for?*   (spear points)
_____ *Why were arrowheads rarely used for arrows?*   (they were too large)

Interpretive question: *Why was the making of early tools a difficult task?*
       Acceptable answer: _____ Yes   _____ No
Memories: _____ Unprompted + _____ Prompted = _____ Total
Organized retelling: _____ Yes   _____ No
Oral reading inaccuracies changed meaning: _____ Yes _____ No
Rate appropriate: _____ Yes _____ No   Fluency appropriate: _____ Yes _____ No
       _____ reads word by word   _____ reads in phrases   _____ good use of punctuation
       _____ good use of stress, pitch, and intonation
Oral reading:
       _____ Substitutions   _____ Mispronunciations
       _____ Additions   _____ Repetitions
       _____ Omissions   _____ Words pronounced by examiner

INSTRUCTIONAL LEVEL GUIDE   Prepared: 4 or fewer errors   Unprepared: 10 or fewer errors   5 or more memories

GRADED PASSAGE (6C/A)

Assessing and Activating Background Knowledge
Here is a story about the constellations. What are star constellations?

_____ Adequate   _____ Inadequate

Motivating Statement   *Read the story to learn more about the constellations and how they help us.*

CONSTELLATIONS

People all over the world have looked at the stars and have seen patterns that reminded them of everyday things. A group of stars that forms such a pattern is a constellation. A constellation lies within a definite region of the sky. By knowing the positions of the constellations, one can locate stars, planets, comets, and other galaxies. There are eighty-eight officially recognized constellations.

Many of the ancient names for certain constellations are still used today, though the things they were named for are no longer a part of our everyday experiences.

Almost anyone who grew up in the Northern Hemisphere can point out the Little Dipper. The Little Dipper is part of the constellation Ursa Minor, which means Little Bear.

Ursa Minor appears to circle the North Star. It is visible all year long. Some groups of stars are only visible during certain seasons of the year.

There are twelve seasonal constellations that are especially important because the sun and the moon always rise within one of their patterns. These are the constellations of the Zodiac.

Constellations are used in ship and airplane navigation. Astronauts use them to help orient spacecraft.

(192 words)

Comprehension Questions

_____ *What do the patterns in the stars remind people of?*   (everyday things)
_____ *What is a constellation?*   (a group of stars that form a pattern)
_____ *How many constellations are there?*   (88)
_____ *What can most people in the Northern Hemisphere identify?*   (Little Dipper)
_____ *What does Ursa Minor mean?*   (Little Bear)
_____ *What constellation appears to circle the North Star?*   (Ursa Minor)
_____ *When is Ursa Minor visible?*   (all year long)
_____ *What does visible mean?*   (able to be seen)
_____ *How many seasonal constellations are there?*   (12)
_____ *How are constellations used?*   (navigation of ships and airplanes, to orient spacecraft)

Interpretive question: *Why do the constellations hold mystery for some people?*
      Acceptable answer: _____ Yes   _____ No
Memories: _____ Unprompted + _____ Prompted = _____ Total
Organized retelling: _____ Yes   _____ No
Oral reading inaccuracies changed meaning: _____ Yes   _____ No
Rate appropriate: _____ Yes   _____ No   Fluency appropriate: _____ Yes   _____ No
      _____ reads word by word   _____ reads in phrases   _____ good use of punctuation
      _____ good use of stress, pitch, and intonation
Oral reading:
      _____ Substitutions   _____ Mispronunciations
      _____ Additions   _____ Repetitions
      _____ Omissions   _____ Words pronounced by examiner

INSTRUCTIONAL LEVEL GUIDE   Prepared: 4 or fewer errors   Unprepared: 10 or fewer errors   6 or more memories

GRADED PASSAGE (6A)

Assessing and Activating Background Knowledge

Here is a story about driver's license requirements. Why is it necessary to have a license to drive?

_____ Adequate   _____ Inadequate

Motivating Statement   *Read the story to learn more about license requirements and important information about driving.*

DRIVER'S LICENSES

States vary in their requirements for a driver's license. Some will give a license to persons sixteen years of age, while others will not. Usually the consent of a parent or guardian is needed if an applicant is under eighteen.

Generally, people need to fulfill three important requirements to get a driver's license. Drivers have to prove skills in driving a vehicle and knowledge of rules and safety procedures. They also have to be physically capable of safe driving. For example, people who are nearsighted are often issued restricted licenses. This means that they must wear glasses or contact lenses when they drive.

Responsible people drive carefully to avoid hurting others or themselves. Most of us realize that having a driver's license suspended or revoked can be very inconvenient. This is especially true when driving is needed for daily commuting to work.

Some states have a system of points. This means that for every violation the driver has, there are so many points are held against him or her. If a driver has too many points in a particular period, the license to drive will be suspended. The system seems helpful since people don't want to lose their driving privileges.   (200 words)

Comprehension Questions

_____ *How do states differ in their age requirements for a driver's license?*   (some issue licenses at 16; others won't)

_____ *Whose consent is needed if the applicant is under eighteen?*   (parent or guardian)

_____ *What are the three requirements necessary to obtain a driver's license?*   (skill in driving, knowledge of rules, physically able to drive)

_____ *What is a restricted license?*   (for those who must wear glasses and so on)

_____ *What is a violation?*   (breaking the law—and the driver receives a ticket)

_____ *Explain the point system used in some states.*   (points are assessed against your license for violations; if too many points are received within a certain time, your license is suspended)

_____ *Why is the system helpful?*   (keeps people thinking about their responsibility behind the wheel—people don't want to lose their licenses)

_____ *Why is having your driver's license revoked an inconvenience?*   (can't do the normal things that you would do with a license)

Interpretive question: *Why is it important to have only responsible people driving cars?*

Acceptable answer: _____ Yes _____ No

Memories: _____ Unprompted + _____ Prompted = _____ Total

Organized retelling: _____ Yes _____ No

Oral reading inaccuracies changed meaning: _____ Yes _____ No

Rate appropriate: _____ Yes _____ No   Fluency appropriate: _____ Yes _____ No

_____ reads word by word   _____ reads in phrases   _____ good use of punctuation
_____ good use of stress, pitch, and intonation

Oral reading:

_____ Substitutions   _____ Mispronunciations
_____ Additions   _____ Repetitions
_____ Omissions   _____ Words pronounced by examiner

INSTRUCTIONAL LEVEL GUIDE   Prepared: 4 or fewer errors   Unprepared: 10 or fewer errors   5 or more memories

GRADED PASSAGE (7C)

Assessing and Activating Background Knowledge

Here is a story about volcanoes. Tell me what you know about volcanoes.

_____ Adequate   _____ Inadequate

Motivating Statement   *Read the story to learn how volcanoes are created and what happens to them.*

VOLCANOES

Powerful forces within the earth cause volcanoes. Scientists do not fully understand these forces. But they have developed theories on how the forces create volcanoes.

A volcano begins deep in the earth, where it is hot enough to melt rock. The molten rock is mixed with gases and floats up through the solid rock around it. Where the earth's crust is weakest, the liquid rock sometimes channels through it and explodes onto the surface in a volcanic eruption.

The melted rock is magma when it is still within the earth. But once it reaches the earth's surface, it is lava.

The lava flows out of the central channel and smaller side channels in streams or in sheets that overlap each other like waves on a beach.

The main gas released by a volcano is steam. Because the steam contains volcanic dust, it looks like smoke.

When the magma is sticky, rock fragments of various sizes are also thrown off by the explosion. The largest fragments are called *bombs*.

The material brought to the surface during a volcanic eruption sometimes forms a mountain around the opening of the central channel. A mountain that was formed by a volcano will have a large, bowl-like crater in its center, and it is also called a volcano.   (213 words)

Comprehension Questions

_____ *Where does a volcano begin?*   (deep in the earth)
_____ *What is molten rock?*   (rock so hot that it has melted)
_____ *How does the molten rock reach the surface?*   (channels through weak places in the earth's surface)
_____ *What is magma?*   (melted rock below earth's surface)
_____ *What is magma called when it reaches the earth's surface?*   (lava)
_____ *What is the main gas released by a volcano?*   (steam)
_____ *Why is this gas the color of smoke?*   (contains volcanic dust)
_____ *What happens when the magma is sticky?*   (rock fragments are thrown off by the explosion)
_____ *What are these fragments called?*   (bombs)
_____ *What is a crater?*   (bowl-like structure in the middle of the volcano)

Interpretive question: *Why can volcanoes be dangerous?*
        Acceptable answer: _____ Yes _____ No
Memories: _____ Unprompted + _____ Prompted = _____ Total
Organized retelling: _____ Yes _____ No
Oral reading inaccuracies changed meaning: _____ Yes _____ No
Rate appropriate: _____ Yes _____ No   Fluency appropriate: _____ Yes _____ No
        _____ reads word by word   _____ reads in phrases   _____ good use of punctuation
        _____ good use of stress, pitch, and intonation
Oral reading:
        _____ Substitutions   _____ Mispronunciations
        _____ Additions   _____ Repetitions
        _____ Omissions   _____ Words pronounced by examiner

INSTRUCTIONAL LEVEL GUIDE   Prepared: 4 or fewer errors   Unprepared: 11 or fewer errors   6 or more memories

GRADED PASSAGE (7C/A)

Assessing and Activating Background Knowledge

Here is a story about dinosaurs. What do you know about them?

_____ Adequate   _____ Inadequate

Motivating Statement   *Read the story to learn an interesting discovery about dinosaurs.*

QUESTIONS ABOUT DINOSAURS

Since the first dinosaur fossils were discovered, scientists have been curious about how they lived. One question was, did dinosaurs take care of their young? We know that dinosaurs laid eggs. Ducks lay eggs and they raise their young ducklings. But turtles lay eggs and, when the eggs hatch, the young turtles are on their own. When we think about birds, snakes, alligators, and other creatures that lay eggs, we can see that some care for their young and others do not.

The question about dinosaurs was answered when scientists found dinosaur footprints with the large prints on the outer circle and very small footprints on the inside. This discovery meant that the adult dinosaurs were protecting the young ones. If you have seen reports on elephants, you probably know that this is exactly what adult elephants do. They form a circle with each elephant in the herd facing outward so they can see lions or other animals approaching them. The tiny young elephants are safe inside the circle.

Scientists continue to ask questions, look for clues, and try to interpret what they find. Because dinosaurs were very different from each other in size, eating habits, and other ways, we don't know if all dinosaurs raised their young. Many questions have been answered about dinosaurs, but more questions remain.   (216 words)

Comprehension Questions

_____ *What question did scientists have about dinosaurs?*   (did they take care of their young)

_____ *Did dinosaurs lay eggs?*   (yes)

_____ *Do all creatures that lay eggs raise their young?*   (no)

_____ *Which egg layers raise their young?*   (ducks)

_____ *Which egg layers do not raise their young?*   (turtles)

_____ *How did the dinosaur footprints answer the scientists' question?*   (the tiny footprints of the young were inside the circle of adult footprints)

_____ *What animals alive today protect their young inside a circle?*   (elephants)

_____ *Do we know if all dinosaurs cared for their young? Why or why not?*   (no, different in size, eating habits, etc.)

Interpretive question: *How do scientists get most of their information about dinosaurs?*

Acceptable answer: _____ Yes   _____ No

Memories: _____ Unprompted + _____ Prompted = _____ Total

Organized retelling: _____ Yes   _____ No

Oral reading inaccuracies changed meaning: _____ Yes   _____ No

Rate appropriate: _____ Yes   _____ No   Fluency appropriate: _____ Yes   _____ No

        _____ reads word by word   _____ reads in phrases   _____ good use of punctuation

        _____ good use of stress, pitch, and intonation

Oral reading:

        _____ Substitutions   _____ Mispronunciations

        _____ Additions   _____ Repetitions

        _____ Omissions   _____ Words pronounced by examiner

INSTRUCTIONAL LEVEL GUIDE   Prepared: 4 or fewer errors   Unprepared: 11 or fewer errors   6 or more memories

GRADED PASSAGE (7A)

Assessing and Activating Background Knowledge

Here is a story about getting a job. Why is a job application important in getting a job?

_____ Adequate   _____ Inadequate

Motivating Statement   *Read the story to learn more about the job application.*

THE JOB APPLICATION

Tina wanted a job in an office. A magazine publishing company had some openings, so Tina went to the personnel department. The receptionist gave her an application form and asked her to go into the next room and complete it. The form was only two pages long, but it had several parts. At the top of the first page, Tina had to write her name, address, and social security number. She was glad that she had put her social security card in her wallet. Next Tina was asked about her record of business experience. That part was easy too, except for the box that said, "Reason for separation." Tina was puzzled, but then she realized they were asking why she had lost her other job. She thought she could explain why she left, but Tina didn't know how she could write the reason in such a tiny box.

The last part of the application asked for three references' names, occupations, and addresses. Tina could not remember the addresses of her references. She didn't know whether to leave that part blank or come back later. Then she had a better idea. Tina used the telephone directory to find the correct addresses. Tina decided that before she applied for any more jobs, she would write down the kind of information needed on applications and take it with her.   (226 words)

Comprehension Questions

_____ *Where did Tina apply for a job?*   (at a magazine publishing company)
_____ *Where did she go when she went to the publishing company?*   (receptionist in personnel office)
_____ *What was she told to do?*   (go to next room and fill out application form)
_____ *On the first page, what information did Tina have to know?*   (name, address, and social security number)
_____ *What else was she asked about?*   (record of business experience)
_____ *What does "reason for separation" mean?*   (reason for leaving her job)
_____ *Why was this a problem?*   (first she couldn't understand the question; then she couldn't explain the reason in such a small space)
_____ *What did the last part of the application ask for?*   (three references)
_____ *How did she find the addresses?*   (looked in the phone book)
_____ *What will she do from now on when she applies for a job?*   (write down information needed and take it with her)

Interpretive question: *If a box on a form is too small, what might an applicant do to provide complete information?*
      Acceptable answer: _____ Yes   _____ No
Memories: _____ Unprompted + _____ Prompted = _____ Total
Organized retelling: _____ Yes   _____ No
Oral reading inaccuracies changed meaning: _____ Yes   _____ No
Rate appropriate: _____ Yes   _____ No   Fluency appropriate: _____ Yes   _____ No
      _____ reads word by word   _____ reads in phrases   _____ good use of punctuation
      _____ good use of stress, pitch, and intonation
Oral reading:
      _____ Substitutions   _____ Mispronunciations
      _____ Additions   _____ Repetitions
      _____ Omissions   _____ Words pronounced by examiner

INSTRUCTIONAL LEVEL GUIDE   Prepared: 5 or fewer errors   Unprepared: 11 or fewer errors   6 or more memories

GRADED PASSAGE (8C)

Assessing and Activating Background Knowledge

What reasons might men have to use a raft?

_____ Adequate   _____ Inadequate

Motivating Statement   *Read the story to learn about a voyage made on a raft.*

KON-TIKI

In 1947, six men set out to cross the Pacific Ocean from Peru to Polynesia—4,300 miles of open ocean—on a raft! This was the famous *Kon-Tiki* expedition, led by Thor Heyerdahl, a Norwegian archaeologist.

These men were attempting to prove that the people of Polynesia had originally come from Peru by crossing the ocean on a raft and that they had been led by a man called Kon-Tiki. Since no one would believe that it was possible to make such a voyage, these six decided to show that it was. They built a raft similar to the ancient Peruvian ones. They took no modern equipment except for a small radio. Nothing steered their craft besides the wind and current; yet they succeeded in making the crossing.

Erik Hesselberg, the only licensed sailor on board, was the navigator of the raft, which was named *Kon-Tiki*. He was also an accomplished artist. He brought along a bottle of ink. He sketched a little every day on the raft in order to have a record for his friends and family.   (179 words)

Comprehension Questions

_____ *In what year did the* Kon-Tiki *expedition take place?*   (1947)
_____ *How many miles did the trip involve?*   (4,300)
_____ *Who led the expedition?*   (Thor Heyerdahl)
_____ *What theory was the expedition trying to prove?*   (that the people of Polynesia had originally come from Peru)
_____ *What provisions did they take on the raft?*   (no modern equipment—just a radio)
_____ *Who was Erik Hesselberg?*   (the only licensed sailor on board)
_____ *What did he do every day aboard the raft?*   (sketched a little every day about the expedition)

Interpretive question: *Why would it be important to keep a diary of happenings on an expedition such as the* Kon-Tiki?

Acceptable answer: _____ Yes   _____ No
Memories: _____ Unprompted + _____ Prompted = _____ Total
Organized retelling: _____ Yes   _____ No
Oral reading inaccuracies changed meaning: _____ Yes   _____ No
Rate appropriate: _____ Yes   _____ No   Fluency appropriate: _____ Yes   _____ No
      _____ reads word by word   _____ reads in phrases   _____ good use of punctuation
      _____ good use of stress, pitch, and intonation
Oral reading:
      _____ Substitutions   _____ Mispronunciations
      _____ Additions   _____ Repetitions
      _____ Omissions   _____ Words pronounced by examiner

INSTRUCTIONAL LEVEL GUIDE   Prepared: 4 or fewer errors   Unprepared: 9 or fewer errors   5 or more memories

GRADED PASSAGE (8C/A)

Assessing and Activating Background Knowledge
Why do people use a catalog to shop?
____ Adequate   ____ Inadequate

Motivating Statement   *Read the story to learn more about mail-order shopping.*

A SHOPPING TRIP

Gene and Kim had been shopping for equipment for their camping trip. For several days they had been going from store to store looking for things they needed. Shopping was taking a lot of time and was very inconvenient. Their neighbor said that he had been shopping by sending for things through a mail-order catalog for years. Gene said that he had heard about mail-order shopping, but he was worried about getting their money back if something was wrong with their purchase. When the neighbor told Gene and Kim that the store offered a refund guarantee, they asked him if they could borrow his catalog.

Kim noticed that people could order merchandise three ways. They could place a telephone order, or mail an order form, or go to the mail-order counter of the store. Because the nearest mail-order store was far away from them, they planned to order by mail.

Gene felt that they had not completely wasted their time by looking through department stores because they could compare the catalog prices with the prices of items they had seen. They were both pleased to find that the measurements of hiking boots were given so that they would be able to tell whether they would fit.   (206 words)

Comprehension Questions
____ What had Kim and Gene been shopping for?   (a camping trip)
____ Why didn't they like to shop?   (takes a lot of time; inconvenient)
____ How had their neighbor been doing his shopping?   (through a mail-order catalog)
____ What is a refund guarantee?   (you can get your money back)
____ Why was Gene skeptical of using a mail-order catalog?   (he was worried about getting his money back if they weren't satisfied)
____ What were the three ways that one could order from a catalog?   (in the store, by phone, or by mail)
____ Which method did Gene and Kim decide to use?   (they ordered by mail)
____ Why did Gene feel they had not wasted their time?   (they could compare prices to those they had found in the catalog)
____ What were they pleased to find in the catalog?   (measurements for boots were given)
____ Why was this important?   (they could tell if they would fit)

Interpretive question: *Why is it important to take your time when you shop?*
    Acceptable answer: ____ Yes ____ No
Memories: ____ Unprompted + ____ Prompted = ____ Total
Organized retelling: ____ Yes ____ No
Oral reading inaccuracies changed meaning: ____ Yes ____ No
Rate appropriate: ____ Yes ____ No   Fluency appropriate: ____ Yes ____ No
    ____ reads word by word   ____ reads in phrases   ____ good use of punctuation
    ____ good use of stress, pitch, and intonation
Oral reading:
    ____ Substitutions   ____ Mispronunciations
    ____ Additions   ____ Repetitions
    ____ Omissions   ____ Words pronounced by examiner

INSTRUCTIONAL LEVEL GUIDE   Prepared: 4 or fewer errors   Unprepared: 11 or fewer errors   6 or more memories

GRADED PASSAGE (8A)

Assessing and Activating Background Knowledge

Here is a story about filling out a job application for a factory. What kind of information do you think was asked for?

_____ Adequate   _____ Inadequate

Motivating Statement *Read the story to learn about the job application form.*

A NEW JOB

Maria was interested in a job in a canning factory. She did not have much work experience, but her brother had a good job in the factory as a supervisor. Maria remembered that he had not had any experience when he started to work there.

At the personnel office, Maria was given an application form to fill out. There was a section that listed several physical problems such as rheumatism, dermatitis, and back trouble. Maria had not heard of some of the conditions, but she decided that if she didn't know what they were, she didn't have a problem with them.

Next, Maria had to check the times she was willing to work: day shift, second shift, or third shift. Because she was taking a class in adult education in the evening, she decided to check day shift and third shift. Maria hoped for the day shift, but she realized that, as a new employee without seniority, she would probably get the third shift.

Finally, Maria filled in the part of the form that asked about apprentice training. She had just finished a vocational training program that had given her some experience, so she was happy to fill in that part.

When Maria returned the completed form, she was told that she would be notified within two weeks about her employment with the company.   (224 words)

Comprehension Questions

_____ *Where did Maria want to work?*   (in a canning factory)
_____ *Who did she know that worked there?*   (her brother)
_____ *What might hinder Maria in getting the job?*   (no experience)
_____ *What was Maria given at the personnel office?*   (an application form)
_____ *What trouble did Maria have in filling out the form?*   (hadn't heard of some of the physical conditions)
_____ *What times did Maria say she was able to work?*   (day and third shift)
_____ *Why was she restricted in the times she could work?*   (she took an adult education class in the evening)
_____ *What experience did she have to add to her application?*   (she had just finished a vocational training program)
_____ *How long would it be before she was notified about the job?*   (within two weeks)
_____ *What is seniority?*   (length of time you have been with a company)

Interpretive question: *Why is it important to be flexible with time when applying for a new job?*
        Acceptable answer: _____ Yes   _____ No
Memories: _____ Unprompted + _____ Prompted = _____ Total
Organized retelling: _____ Yes   _____ No
Oral reading inaccuracies changed meaning: _____ Yes   _____ No
Rate appropriate: _____ Yes   _____ No   Fluency appropriate: _____ Yes   _____ No
        _____ reads word by word   _____ reads in phrases   _____ good use of punctuation
        _____ good use of stress, pitch, and intonation
Oral reading:
        _____ Substitutions   _____ Mispronunciations
        _____ Additions   _____ Repetitions
        _____ Omissions   _____ Words pronounced by examiner

INSTRUCTIONAL LEVEL GUIDE   Prepared: 5 or fewer errors   Unprepared: 11 or fewer errors   6 or more memories

GRADED PASSAGE (9–10C)

Assessing and Activating Background Knowledge

This passage is about chemistry. Tell me anything you know about chemistry.

_____ Adequate   _____ Inadequate

Motivating Statement   *Read the story to learn about a modern discovery in chemistry.*

MODERN CHEMISTRY

One of the founders of modern chemistry was a wealthy Frenchman, Antoine Lavoisier, who lived in the late eighteenth century. Lavoisier burned different substances in a closed chamber and proved that there was no change in their weight. This showed that the basic elements remained the same even though their appearance was completely altered.

To explain this phenomenon, an English chemist, John Dalton, proposed the atomic theory in 1810. According to Dalton's theory, all matter is composed of minute building blocks, which he called *atoms*. The atoms of the different elements vary in size and characteristics. Though the elements themselves can and do combine to form new substances, their atoms always remain the same.

Guided by this theory, a Russian scientist, Dmitri Mendelyeev, arranged all of the known elements in a table according to their atomic weights. He showed that the elements fell naturally into certain groups with similar properties. Since many gaps appeared in the table, chemists began to search for the missing elements.

The field of science contains many examples of discoveries being shared by people from different nations. Because lack of communication can be disastrous to the growth of knowledge, most scientists are eager to compare results and learn from each other.   (205 words)

Comprehension Questions

_____ *Who was one of the founders of modern chemistry?*   (Antoine Lavoisier)

_____ *What important discovery did he make?*   (basic elements remained the same even though there was a change in appearance)

_____ *Who proposed the atomic theory?*   (John Dalton)

_____ *In what year was this theory proposed?*   (1810)

_____ *What term did he use to describe atoms?*   (building blocks)

_____ *How do atoms vary?*   (in size and characteristics)

_____ *Who arranged the elements in a table?*   (Dmitri Mendelyeev)

_____ *What did the table show?*   (elements fell naturally into certain groups)

_____ *What did chemists start searching for?*   (the missing elements)

Interpretive question: *Why is experimentation so important to a field like chemistry?*

    Acceptable answer: _____ Yes _____ No

Memories: _____ Unprompted + _____ Prompted = _____ Total

Organized retelling: _____ Yes _____ No

Oral reading inaccuracies changed meaning: _____ Yes _____ No

Rate appropriate: _____ Yes _____ No   Fluency appropriate: _____ Yes   _____ No

    _____ reads word by word   _____ reads in phrases   _____ good use of punctuation

    _____ good use of stress, pitch, and intonation

Oral reading:

    _____ Substitutions   _____ Mispronunciations

    _____ Additions   _____ Repetitions

    _____ Omissions   _____ Words pronounced by examiner

INSTRUCTIONAL LEVEL GUIDE   Prepared: 4 or fewer errors   Unprepared: 10 or fewer errors   6 or more memories

GRADED PASSAGE (9–10C/A)

Assessing and Activating Background Knowledge

This passage is about translating one language into another. What are some problems in translating?

_____ Adequate   _____ Inadequate

Motivating Statement   *Read the story to learn more about translating.*

A FAILURE TO COMMUNICATE

When two people speak the same first language, they occasionally misunderstand each other. Imagine the difficulties that interpreters have when they must first understand what the speaker of one language has said and then translate the message into another language.

Translators are challenged when the speaker makes a reference to an event or story character that is not known to listeners from another country. A speaker may refer to someone as a "Cinderella," meaning that a person was once poor and is now wealthy, but if the listeners do not know the story, the meaning is lost.

Translating quickly, while the first person is speaking, is especially difficult. Yet, simultaneous translation is used today in about 85 percent of all international meetings. Not only are translators working with the United Nations, but they are employed for business, scientific, and educational meetings as well.

Computers are being programmed to translate languages. Although computers have great potential for speedy translations, they have some of the same problems that human translators have. In an early attempt to translate English into Russian, a computer translated, "out of sight, out of mind," as "invisible idiot."

In our global society we need to work hard to understand each other and keep a sense of humor.   (209 words)

Comprehension Questions

_____ *What does a translator do?*   (take a message from one language and give it to someone in another language)
_____ *What kinds of challenges do translators have?*   (translating a reference to events or stories unknown to the listeners)
_____ (translating quickly or simultaneously)
_____ *What is meant by referring to someone as "Cinderella"?*   (someone who was poor and is now wealthy)
_____ *Where are translators employed?*   (United Nations, business, scientific, educational meetings)
_____ *What percentage of international meetings use translators?*   (85 percent)
_____ *What problem did a computer have in translating?*   (gave literal translation for a proverb; "out of sight, out of mind" translated as "invisible idiot")
_____ *What does our global society require?*   (work to understand each other and have a sense of humor)

Interpretive question: *Why do people who speak the same language have trouble understanding each other sometimes?*

        Acceptable answer: _____ Yes _____ No
Memories: _____ Unprompted + _____ Prompted = _____ Total
Organized retelling: _____ Yes _____ No
Oral reading inaccuracies changed meaning: _____ Yes _____ No
Rate appropriate: _____ Yes _____ No   Fluency appropriate: _____ Yes _____ No
        _____ reads word by word   _____ reads in phrases   _____ good use of punctuation
        _____ good use of stress, pitch, and intonation
 Oral reading:
        _____ Substitutions   _____ Mispronunciations
        _____ Additions   _____ Repetitions
        _____ Omissions   _____ Words pronounced by examiner

INSTRUCTIONAL LEVEL GUIDE   Prepared: 4 or fewer errors   Unprepared: 11 or fewer errors   6 or more memories

GRADED PASSAGE (9–10A)

Assessing and Activating Background Knowledge

This passage is about a voter drive. Why is a voter drive important before an election?

_____ Adequate   _____ Inadequate

Motivating Statement   *Read the story to learn more about how a voter drive helps with registration.*

VOTER DRIVE

Soon after Jim moved to Plainfield, he received a telephone call from a person who asked if he was registered to vote in the coming election. Jim said that he hadn't thought about it. The caller said she was a member of a local organization that was sponsoring a voter drive. She didn't represent any particular political party but only wanted to encourage people to register and to vote.

Since registration terms and procedures differ from one part of the country to another, the people working in the voter drive offered to explain the local procedures and tell people where they could register.

The caller explained that after Jim registered, he would be mailed a sample ballot for each election. The ballot would contain the names of the candidates and the measures to be voted on.

Jim asked some questions and then thanked the caller for giving him information about voter registration.

Frequently people say that they don't bother to vote because one vote is not significant. Jim read that a presidential election, referred to as the Revolution of 1800, resulted in Burr and Jefferson having the same number of votes. Jim appreciated being reminded about voter registration when he recalled that important tie.
(204 words)

Comprehension Questions

_____ *From whom did Jim receive a phone call?*   (a person from a local organization)
_____ *Why was she calling?*   (she was encouraging people to vote and register)
_____ *What did the caller want Jim to do?*   (register to vote)
_____ *What services was she providing?*   (explaining the local procedures and telling people where to vote)
_____ *After he registers, what will he receive in the mail?*   (sample ballot)
_____ *Why would that information be helpful?*   (the ballot would contain the names of candidates and measures to be voted on; one could read and study to know the candidates and issues by the election)
_____ *How does voting differ from one part of the country to another?*   (procedures and registration forms)
_____ *Why did Jim know one vote could be important?*   (remembered Burr-Jefferson tie)

Interpretive question: *Why is it important to inform yourself about the candidates and issues before you vote?*
       Acceptable answer: _____ Yes   _____ No
Memories: _____ Unprompted + _____ Prompted = _____ Total
Organized retelling: _____ Yes   _____ No
Oral reading inaccuracies changed meaning: _____ Yes   _____ No
Rate appropriate: _____ Yes   _____ No   Fluency appropriate: _____ Yes   _____ No
       _____ reads word by word   _____ reads in phrases   _____ good use of punctuation
       _____ good use of stress, pitch, and intonation
Oral reading:
       _____ Substitutions   _____ Mispronunciations
       _____ Additions   _____ Repetitions
       _____ Omissions   _____ Words pronounced by examiner

INSTRUCTIONAL LEVEL GUIDE   Prepared: 4 or fewer errors   Unprepared: 10 or fewer errors   5 or more memories

GRADED PASSAGE (11–12C)

Assessing and Activating Background Knowledge
Tell me about any of your favorite kinds of paintings.
_____ Adequate   _____ Inadequate

Motivating Statement   *Read the story to learn more about Impressionist art.*

IMPRESSIONISTS

Many schools of modern art have arisen, but we have space to describe only a few. The earliest group, the Impressionists, sought to capture on canvas the impression a person gets when he looks at a scene casually. They therefore merely sketched in the main features in bold brush strokes, allowing the observer's mind to fill in the details. Similarly, they did not mix pigments on a palette in the traditional style. Instead, they used dabs of the basic colors that the viewer's eye blends to form the desired shades. Examined at close range, the Impressionists' paintings seem a blotch of colors and forms. But when the viewer steps back, they suddenly seem to come alive.

The Impressionists' work, unlike more conventional paintings, generally appeared rather flat. The founder of the post-Impressionist school, Paul Cezanne, experimented for years to remedy this weakness. He finally succeeded, by distorting the shapes of objects and using thick layers of carefully blended colors, in creating on canvas the illusion of solidity and depth.

While one may prefer a particular school of painting, an attempt should be made to understand several approaches to visual interpretations and expressions. The rewards are several: a fresh perspective, an understanding of others, and an enrichment of the aesthetic senses.   (210 words)

Comprehension Questions

_____ *What did the Impressionists try to capture on canvas?*   (what a person sees when he looks casually at a scene)
_____ *Who filled in the details of a painting?*   (the observer's mind)
_____ *What is the traditional style of mixing pigments?*   (using a palette)
_____ *What do Impressionist paintings resemble at close range?*   (a blotch of colors)
_____ *Who was the founder of the post-Impressionistic school?*   (Paul Cezanne)
_____ *What was the weakness of Impressionistic work?*   (it appeared flat)
_____ *How did Cezanne succeed in remedying this weakness?*   (distorting shapes, using thick layers of colors)

Interpretive question: *Why is appreciating art a matter of opinion and taste?*
        Acceptable answer: _____ Yes   _____ No
Memories: _____ Unprompted + _____ Prompted = _____ Total
Organized retelling: _____ Yes   _____ No
Oral reading inaccuracies changed meaning: _____ Yes   _____ No
Rate appropriate: _____ Yes   _____ No   Fluency appropriate: _____ Yes   _____ No
        _____ reads word by word   _____ reads in phrases   _____ good use of punctuation
        _____ good use of stress, pitch, and intonation
Oral reading:
        _____ Substitutions   _____ Mispronunciations
        _____ Additions   _____ Repetitions
        _____ Omissions   _____ Words pronounced by examiner

INSTRUCTIONAL LEVEL GUIDE   Prepared: 4 or fewer errors   Unprepared: 10 or fewer errors   5 or more memories

GRADED PASSAGE (11–12C/A)

Assessing and Activating Background Knowledge

This passage is about global warfare. What does global warfare mean?

_____ Adequate   _____ Inadequate

Motivating Statement   *Read the story to learn about how global warfare has affected our country.*

GLOBAL WARFARE

Soon after it reached the White House, news of the attack on Pearl Harbor was broadcast to the American people. Many will never forget hearing newscasters breaking in on symphony concerts, football games, and children's programs to tell of the awful event. The next day the president asked Congress to accept the "state of war" that Japan's "unprovoked and dastardly attack" had thrust upon the United States; Congress accepted the challenge without dissent.

Although a brilliant military feat, the attack on Pearl Harbor eventually proved to be a colossal blunder on the part of the Japanese. To be sure, it cleared the way for an easy conquest of the Philippines and the East Indies by crippling the American naval forces in the Pacific. But the unprovoked attack united the American people as almost nothing else could have done. In their anger they forgot the bitter partisan quarrels over foreign policies and thought only how to best win a war that no one had wanted.

Subsequent analysis of the political and economic policies that contributed to the outbreak of war revealed that the events that culminated in the great war in the Pacific were the result of many factors.

After hostilities ended, both countries worked toward a harmonious relationship.

When World War II ended, representatives from many nations worked through the United Nations to develop mechanisms for avoiding the recurrence of another nightmare of violence, death, and destruction. Yet wars have continued to occur. The fighting in Southeast Asia and in the Middle East has horrified people who hoped never to see more bloodshed. Nations struggle against nations for economic, political, and cultural reasons. Resolution of complex problems is slow; yet it must come. Another global conflict, with or without the nuclear holocaust, must be avoided.   (295 words)

Comprehension Questions

_____ *How did the president describe the attack?*   (unprovoked and dastardly)
_____ *How did Congress react to the actions of Japan?*   (declared war immediately)
_____ *Why was this attack considered a "colossal blunder"?*   (it united the American people)
_____ *Why was the attack a "brilliant military feat"?*   (cleared the way for an easy conquest of the Philippines and East Indies)
_____ *Which American forces were crippled?*   (naval)
_____ *What does the word* partisan *mean?*   (taking one side)
_____ *What had the American people been quarreling about?*   (foreign policies)
_____ *What kind of factors contributed to the cause of the war?*   (political and economic)

Interpretive question: *Why are there partisan quarrels over foreign policy?*
        Acceptable answer: _____ Yes _____ No
Memories: _____ Unprompted + _____ Prompted = _____ Total   Organized retelling: _____ Yes _____ No
Oral reading inaccuracies changed meaning: _____ Yes _____ No
Rate appropriate: _____ Yes _____ No   Fluency appropriate: _____ Yes _____ No
        _____ reads word by word   _____ reads in phrases   _____ good use of punctuation
        _____ good use of stress, pitch, and intonation
Oral reading:
        _____ Substitutions   _____ Mispronunciations
        _____ Additions   _____ Repetitions
        _____ Omissions   _____ Words pronounced by examiner

INSTRUCTIONAL LEVEL GUIDE   **Prepared: 6 or fewer errors   Unprepared: 14 or fewer errors   5 or more memories**

GRADED PASSAGE (11–12A)

Assessing and Activating Background Knowledge

This passage is about people's rights. What are some rights you think workers should have?

_____ Adequate   _____ Inadequate

Motivating Statement   *Read the story to learn about how laws to protect these rights came about and why they are important.*

IMPROVEMENT FOR WORKERS

When states first passed laws regulating labor conditions, they ran into a serious difficulty. Employers challenged the laws, claiming that they interfered with a worker's freedom to work on whatever terms he chose. In 1908 a case came before the Supreme Court in which the new progressive point of view on this kind of legislation was first expressed. An Oregon law protecting women workers was called a violation of the due process clause of the Fourteenth Amendment. The lawyer defending the state of Oregon produced pages and pages of evidence to reveal how the health of women would be jeopardized unless they were protected from employers who forced them to endure long hours and paid them a meager wage. The health of women, it was argued, in the long run would affect the welfare of the nation. The Supreme Court declared that the Oregon law was constitutional.

This case was by no means the last time the Fourteenth Amendment was employed in an attempt to block reform legislation. But the decision in favor of Oregon did encourage many states to pass laws protecting labor, and the courts upheld several of them.

During periods of economic stress, pressure is often brought to bear on legislators to repeal laws that protect employees. One argument frequently heard is that by paying wages below the minimum standard, employers can afford to hire more people, thereby decreasing unemployment. Those representing workers are quick to point out that there is no guarantee that employers would expand their hiring and that improving the economy is a better alternative than offering starvation wages. A high standard of living and good working conditions are not easily surrendered.   (278 words)

Comprehension Questions

_____ *Who challenged the states who were trying to regulate labor conditions?*   (the employers)
_____ *Why were the employers challenging these laws?*   (they claimed they interfered with a worker's freedom)
_____ *In what year did a test case come before the Supreme Court?*   (1908)
_____ *Why was the Oregon law challenged?*   (called a violation of due process clause of 14th Amendment)
_____ *What unfair practices were employers charged with?*   (forced women to work long hours for little pay)
_____ *What was the basis of the lawyer's case who was defending Oregon?*   (health of women hurt; this could affect nation)
_____ *Who won the case?*   (Oregon)
_____ *How did this decision affect other states?*   (they passed laws to protect labor also)

Interpretive question: *Why is it important to have good labor conditions?*
        Acceptable answer: _____ Yes _____ No
Memories: _____ Unprompted + _____ Prompted = _____ Total   Organized retelling: _____ Yes   _____ No
Oral reading inaccuracies changed meaning: _____ Yes _____ No
Rate appropriate: _____ Yes _____ No   Fluency appropriate: _____ Yes   _____ No
        _____ reads word by word   _____ reads in phrases   _____ good use of punctuation
        _____ good use of stress, pitch, and intonation
Oral reading:
        _____ Substitutions   _____ Mispronunciations
        _____ Additions   _____ Repetitions
        _____ Omissions   _____ Words pronounced by examiner

INSTRUCTIONAL LEVEL GUIDE   Prepared: 6 or fewer errors   Unprepared: 14 or fewer errors   5 or more memories

SPELLING TESTS

Seven word lists are provided in the Diagnostic Spelling Tests (pp. 82–84) so that the examiner can obtain diagnostic information related to the student's ability to spell. Only ten words are included in each test in order to prevent fatigue or discouragement. Therefore, additional evidence of student performance must be gathered from his or her writing to confirm hypotheses about the student in regard to cognitive development in encoding language; sound-symbol association; auditory discrimination, memory, and sequencing; visual discrimination, memory, and sequencing; and knowledge of common rules and conventions.

ADMINISTRATION

Select only the test or tests that appear to be appropriate to the area being explored and the reading level of the student. For example, give tests one and three to nonreaders and those below the third-grade reading level. Move to easier or more difficult lists as necessary. For each test give the student a separate sheet of lined paper, numbered from one to ten. Say, "*I want you to write some words for me, please. If there are some words you don't know, just try to spell them as well as you can. I will say each word, use it in a sentence, and say it again. Then you are to write the word. Remember to wait until I say the word the last time before you start to write.*" The examiner may repeat the word and encourage the student to "*try it even if you aren't sure*" and "*you can say it as you write it,*" but no other prompting, such as sounding by word parts, is permitted. This test may be administered to groups.

INTERPRETATION

Lists One and Two, Phonetic Spelling

Lists one and two can be used to determine whether students can discriminate sounds, associate sounds with letters, and write sounds in sequence. Students may have memorized some words in these and other lists; consider this in interpretation. In addition to analyzing the student's production, note whether the student said the words or sounds of the letters before, during, or after writing as an aid to production.

Lists Three and Four, Nonphonetic Spelling

Lists three and four can be used to determine whether students can make fine visual discriminations within words, recall visual letter forms, and reproduce them in sequence. Note attempts to visually recall the word before writing to see if it "looks right." These lists may also be used to learn whether the student attempts to recall the word by reciting the names rather than the sounds of the letters before, during, or after writing the words.

Lists Five and Six, Spelling Rules and Conventions

These lists sample students' knowledge of spelling rules and conventions. These can be learned inductively by students who discover patterns in derived words they read and write. Some students may have had some instruction in rules and can be heard reciting, "*i* before *e* . . ." or "change the *y* to *i*. . . ." Words missed on parts reflecting a common spelling pattern should be rechecked by testing with similar words. Those patterns not known may be acquired through practice with similar derived forms. Rules may be useful to those with poor visual discrimination and memory. (Some words on this test may have been memorized by the students and do not reflect their mastery of a spelling rule or convention.)

List Seven, High-Frequency Words Commonly Misspelled

List seven contains words that older students with spelling difficulties often misspell. Because these are high-frequency function words, their use cannot be avoided. Older students may have written these words incorrectly so often that the misspelling no longer appears to be incorrect or different from the correct spelling they see in printed materials. In addition to the 10 words on this list, the examiner should check the student's writing for frequently misspelled words.

SUMMARIZING STUDENT SPELLING PERFORMANCE

The foregoing lists and samples of the student's writing can be used to make a detailed analysis of spelling performance. A checklist for this purpose appears on page 85.

COGNITIVE DEVELOPMENT AS A BASIS FOR SELECTING A REMEDIAL READING APPROACH

In their self-evaluations, practicing teachers, reading specialists, and those completing their master's degree in reading frequently mention the need for more guidelines in selecting an appropriate instructional approach for severely disabled readers. One hesitates to give a simplistic set of rules because of the number of factors that can influence the efficacy of a particular approach (e.g., emotional problems, impaired vision or hearing, language problems, previous instruction, neurological difficulties, and so forth). Nevertheless, some indicators of cognitive development with regard to writing words seem to be helpful to teachers who are planning remediation.

The following case excerpts illustrate a fairly typical kind of analysis that has been useful in deciding whether to try a Fernald Language Experience Approach (LEA) or an alternative approach with certain students with reading difficulties. Table 1 contains the attempts of four children to write the list of words that were dictated to them.

TABLE 1
Words Written from Dictation: Four Children

Words Dictated	JON 8 Yr., 0 Mo. RL: Pp ML: 3.0	TIM 7 Yr., 8 Mo. RL: Pp ML: 2.5	JEFF 8 Yr., 9 Mo. RL: Pp ML: 2.0	TRISHA 7 Yr., 6 Mo. RL: Pp ML: 2.0
1. go	go	po	G	go
2. pad	pD	pd	p	pad
3. set	ct	sct	S	set
4. fed	yD*	ft	f	fed
5. pep	PP	pt	p	pep
6. last	LccD	Lt	L	last
7. find	yD*	fv	f	fid
8. chip	Cep	Pi	—	chip
9. wish	—	A	—	wish
10. bus	Bcc	BS	b	bus

*Consistently wrote y for A.

RL = Reading Level

ML = Math Level

Table 2 contains a guide to the development of the ability to write words. Although ability varies widely from child to child, generally the sequence that can be observed is one that moves from a representation of the first sound in a word, to the addition of the final consonant sound, and finally to the representation of vowels. This progression in children's learning has been described by Henderson and Beers (1980) and others. The author has found that adult beginning readers tend to follow the same sequence.

TABLE 2
Cognitive Development in Writing Words

Approximate Grade Level	Pencil	Bed	Make
K–1.0	P	B	M
1.5	PSL	BD	MK
1.9	PWSL	BAD	MAEK
2.0	PNSAL	BED	MAKE

Jon, Tim, and Jeff have learned to perform simple tasks in addition and subtraction, indicating that they have the ability to learn. They can recognize very few words, but they can discriminate and represent the beginning sound in a word. Jeff, however, has not reached the level of Jon and Tim in word knowledge, since they can write the final sound in some words and Jeff cannot. The three boys have had psychological evaluations that report full-scale IQs from 81 to 90. They are in regular classrooms.

Jon, Tim, and Jeff were guided through the standard VAKT-Language Experience Approach described by Fernald (1943). With only a few trials Jon and Tim were writing words and reading them in their experience stories. Jeff required many trials and needed much support in reading the stories he dictated. It seemed apparent that Jeff's knowledge of words had not developed to the stage where the Fernald approach would be the most effective. Therefore, Jeff was given some structured guidance in the study of one-syllable words. The Hegge, Kirk, and Kirk (1965) word patterns were used, although any similar material would have sufficed. Although initially Jeff needed to keep a picture before him to remind him of the medial vowel sound, he was soon competently sorting words, creating rhymes, and fluently reading the beginning drills. This guided word study helped Jeff move to the level of phonological competence that he needed to be successful in beginning reading instruction.

Trisha was 7 years, 6 months old in the eighth month of first grade. She had been evaluated by the school psychologist, who reported her scores as indicating borderline mental impairment. An occupational therapist described Trisha as functioning slightly below level in development of spatial organization and balance. A speech therapist had been helping Trisha overcome articulation problems. Trisha's major difficulty in the classroom was following directions. The same behavior was noted during testing. She needed repeated explanations, supported with visual aids.

Trisha's reading level in context, oral and silent, and on the word list test was preprimer. She did not use context in reading; given the oral cloze test for beginning readers, Trisha correctly completed only three out of eight. A sample of Trisha's speech was taped and transcribed. She was able to use short sentences correctly, but her language became grammatically incorrect and difficult to understand when she attempted longer sentences. Trisha did well on sentence repetition and syntax matching tests.

On the dictated spelling list, Trisha missed only one word. She omitted the *n* in *find*. The results of the phonics inventory indicated good sound-symbol knowledge. Trisha could discriminate and associate consonants and consonant blends as well as short and long vowels.

Since the major impediment to growth reading seemed to be Trisha's language-processing difficulties, a holistic reading approach was selected that employed neurological impress procedures for the first stage of remediation. After four weeks, Trisha's reading was greatly improved and she was able to move from preprimer to first-grade material. Later, Trisha's fluency and confidence were aided with prepared oral reading as described by Veatch (1978) and participation in choral reading activities. When Trisha started to use LEA, she was given instruction in sentence expansions.

While one hesitates to say that the selection of the remedial approach is limited only to the factors presented here, Jon, Tim, and Jeff are representative of a number of children one sees in the clinical setting. Teachers seem to find the analysis of writing to be helpful in selecting a starting point for instruction for these children.

Children such as Trisha present a difficult challenge. Teachers are puzzled when they see an adequate development of phonological understanding but a lack of development in more holistic processing. Generally, the situation is reversed. For these children, analysis of receptive language, oral language, and written language is required in order to make a decision about remedial approaches.

REFERENCES

References are given for the classic, original descriptions of methodology. Generally, more recent writers condense their presentations of these methods, resulting in the methods not always being used effectively. Readers are encouraged to read original documents as well as more current interpretations and adaptations.

Fernald, G. M. (1943). *Remedial techniques in basic school subjects.* New York: McGraw-Hill.

Heckleman, R. G. (1969). "Using the neurological impress remedial reading technique." *Academic Therapy Quarterly, I*(4).

Hegge, T. G., Kirk, S. A., & Kirk, W. D. (1965). *Remedial reading drills.* Ann Arbor, MI: George Wahr.

Henderson, E., & Beers, J. (Eds.). (1980). *Developmental and cognitive aspects of learning to spell: A reflection of word knowledge.* Newark, DE: International Reading Association.

Veatch, J. (1978). *Reading in the elementary school.* New York: John Wiley and Sons.

Remedial methods mentioned in this section are described in:

Bader, L. A. (1980). *Reading diagnosis and remediation in classroom and clinic.* New York: Macmillan.

Gunning, T. G. (1998). *Assessing and correcting reading and writing difficulties.* Boston: Allyn & Bacon.

Manzo, A. V., & Manzo, U. C. (1993). *Literacy disorders holistic diagnosis and remediation.* Fort Worth, TX: Harcourt Brace Jovanovich.

McCormick, S. (1995). *Instructing students who have literacy problems.* Columbus, OH: Merrill/Prentice Hall.

DIAGNOSTIC SPELLING TESTS

DIRECTIONS: Pronounce the word, use the word in a sentence, and repeat the word.

LIST ONE:
Words Spelled Phonetically, Requiring Ability to Hear and Write Sounds

Reading Levels P–2.0

1. go	Where did he go?
2. pad	I have a pad of paper.
3. sit	Please sit here.
4. fed	I fed my dog.
5. pep	A cheerleader has pep.
6. last	This is my last piece of paper.
7. find	I can't find it.
8. chip	There is a chip out of this cup.
9. wish	Make a wish.
10. bus	We rode the bus.

LIST TWO:
Words Spelled Phonetically, Requiring Ability to Hear and Write Sounds

Reading Levels 3+

1. flash	Here is a flashlight.
2. thump	I heard a thump.
3. wind	The wind blows.
4. strap	The strap broke.
5. twist	Twist the strings together to make a rope.
6. rent	The house is for rent.
7. boots	She put on her boots.
8. child	The child is four years old.
9. split	The man split wood for a fire.
10. mouth	You must take care of the teeth in your mouth.

LIST THREE:
Words with Silent Letters, Requiring Visual Memory

Reading Levels P–2.0

1. one	I have one pencil.
2. eat	Eat an apple.
3. were	We were outside.
4. ice	They have some ice cream.
5. may	May I help you?
6. here	He is not here.
7. happy	They are happy.
8. little	I saw a little dog.
9. come	Come to my house.
10. they	They are not here.

LIST FOUR:
Words with Silent Letters, Requiring Visual Memory

Reading Levels 3+

1. store	We went to the store.
2. listen	Listen to the music.
3. high	How high can you jump?
4. laugh	She made me laugh.
5. write	Will you write me a letter?
6. hour	We were there an hour.
7. know	Do you know how to skate?
8. loaf	I bought a loaf of bread.
9. would	Would you go with me?
10. light	Please turn on the light.

LIST FIVE:
Words Illustrating Common Spelling Rules and Conventions
(may also reflect visual memory)

Reading Levels 2–4

1. stopped	She stopped the car.
2. glasses	Do you wear glasses?
3. coming	He is coming home.
4. flies	My friend flies a plane.
5. cookie	I ate a cookie.
6. cutting	We will be cutting wood.
7. hoped	I hoped you would come.
8. using	Are you using your ruler?
9. finally	We finally went home.
10. beginning	We were beginning to get tired.

LIST SIX:
Words Illustrating Common Spelling Rules and Conventions
(may also reflect visual memory)

Reading Levels 5+

1. equally	The pie was divided equally.
2. musician	The violinist is a fine musician.
3. knives	We need more forks and knives.
4. usefulness	The usefulness of this tool has been established.
5. humorous	The stores were humorous.
6. impression	He tried to make a good impression.
7. receive	Did you receive a letter?
8. factories	The factories are on the edge of town.
9. substantial	She made a substantial investment.
10. immeasurable	The amount was immeasurable.

LIST SEVEN:
High-Frequency Words Commonly Misspelled

Reading Levels 4+

1. been	Where have you been?	
2. when	When will you be ready?	
3. does	How does that work?	
4. were	Were you at the game?	
5. because	He smiled because he was happy.	
6. what	What colors do you like?	
7. know	So you know that person?	
8. many	Many people went to the game.	
9. their	This is their home.	
10. too	We ate too much.	

SUMMARY OF SPELLING PERFORMANCE

Student's name _____   Date _____

Yes/No

_____ Ability to hear and represent sounds developed on level with peers.

    Developmental Stage: _____

    _____ Prephonetic: _____ Scribble: _____ Random letters: _____

    _____ Letter name strategy: _____ Initial letter: _____ 2 or more letters: _____

    _____ Transitional to correct forms: _____

Knowledge of Phonetic Elements

_____ Consonants. Unknown: _____

_____ Vowels. Unknown (long and short): _____

_____ Consonant combinations. Unknown: _____

_____ Vowel combinations. Unknown: _____

Spelling Behaviors   *Examples*

_____ Omits sounded letters _____

_____ Omits silent letters _____

_____ Adds letters, phonetically acceptable _____

_____ Adds letters, not phonetically acceptable _____

_____ Transposes order of silent letters _____

_____ Transposes order of sounded letters _____

_____ Phonetic substitutions, consonants _____

_____ Phonetic substitutions, vowels _____

_____ Nonphonetic substitutions, consonants _____

_____ Nonphonetic substitutions, vowels _____

_____ Substitutions reflect accurate representation of dialect _____

_____

_____ Lacks knowledge of common rules or conventions _____

_____

_____ Needs help with high-frequency words used in writing _____

_____

Examiner's conclusions: _____

_____

_____

(See the Preliteracy Assessment Testing Record on p. 111.)

VISUAL DISCRIMINATION TESTS

Two tests of visual discrimination are provided. They both require the student to match letters and words. The first test, Visual Discrimination I, may be used with nonreaders and beginning readers on levels PP–1. Visual Discrimination II may be used with students reading on level 2 and above.

ADMINISTRATION: Say, *"On this paper you are to look at the letter, word, or phrase after the number, and circle the following items that are the same. In some parts there will be more than one item that is the same; circle them all. First do the practice line (example)."* Give help as needed. When the student understands the task, say, *"Begin."* Time the student unobtrusively. Permit her or him to take as much time as necessary to complete the task.

INTERPRETATION: Note whether the time needed to complete the task and the number of errors are excessive in comparison with peers. Problems may be indicated by holding head close to the page, matching letter by letter, using fingers to hold place, constant rechecking, or erasing. A general guide: PP and level 1 readers should take no more than 3 minutes to complete Visual Discrimination I; Level 2 and above readers should take no more than 3 minutes to complete Visual Discrimination II. The difficulty that nonreaders often have with tasks 7 and 8 may not be related to visual difficulties.

Name _____

VISUAL DISCRIMINATION I

Example: O   K   W   O   X

1. V   N   A   W   V

2. a   g   e   a   o   u   a

3. d   d   p   b   g   d   p   b

4. on   ua   no   om   mo   on

5. saw   mas   saw   was   sam   saw

6. flag   flay   flog   flag   lafg   flay

7. at me   to me   te mo   at we   at me
                ot me   at me   it me   at ne

8. stop the car   stop tha car   stop the cow   stop the car
                    stop the car   pots the car   stod the car
                    stop the rac   stob the car   stop the car

VISUAL DISCRIMINATION II

Example: B   A C B O P X B L M N O B C

1. a   g f j c e a l m n e
             o l b q a b a c x

2. ralg   ralg   role   rall   raly   rolg   raly
             ralg   rolg   raly   rapg   rabg

3. flag   flay   fbly   flag   plag   flug   fbov
             blag   plag   flag   flug   flog

4. Eastern   Andron High   Eastern High   Eostern High   Eastern Heyl
   High   Eistern High   Eastern Hiyl   Eastern High   Eustern High

5. round   ring the bend   round the bowl   round the bend
   the bend round the bind   round thi bend   round tha bend
             rouse the bend   round the bend   round the bend
             around the bend   round the bind   round the pend

6. BEST   BENT   BEST   BENT   BECT   BEST   BEIT
             BEST   BESF   BIST   BEST   BINH

7. everybody   everybody   everydoby   ewerybody   everybaby
                everybody   evevybody   everybody   evarybody

AUDITORY DISCRIMINATION TEST

The Auditory Discrimination of Word Pairs test requires the student to listen to two words to determine if they are alike or different. The examiner can obtain information to help determine whether the student should be referred for a hearing test and whether the student might have difficulty in hearing fine sound differences so that letter-sound association instruction would be impeded.

ADMINISTRATION: Place the student so he or she cannot see the examiner's face. Say, "*I am going to say some words for you. Listen so you can tell me if the words are the same or different.*" If the examiner has reason to doubt the student's understanding of same or different, say, "**Same** *means I said it two times.* **Big, big.** *I said* **big** *two times. They were the same words. Now listen.* **Big, twig.** *I said two* **different words.** *Tell me what same words and different words mean.*" When the student understands same and different, begin the test.

Before giving the test, practice saying the word pairs so that inflection and emphasis are the same on each pair of words. It may be helpful to practice with a tape recorder to ensure a clear enunciation that does not provide clues to the listener.

SCORING AND INTERPRETATION: Total the number of errors. Six-year-old children should make no more than six errors; seven-year-old children, no more than five errors; and those eight years old or older, no more than four errors. This assumes an attentive, cooperative student without a cold, allergy, or other temporary physical problems; optimum, quiet testing conditions; and careful test administration. The examiner may wish to examine the words on which the errors occurred. The letters in front of each word pair indicate the location of the difference: *B*—beginning; *M*—middle; *E*—ending. An *S* is used if the pair is the same. Students with some kinds of high-frequency hearing loss may have difficulty with consonants, especially ending sounds; those with low-frequency loss may have difficulty hearing the middle sounds (vowels). Research indicates that auditory discrimination of speech sounds continues to develop until about the age of eight. Results of this test may indicate the need for further testing of auditory discrimination or testing of auditory acuity.

AUDITORY DISCRIMINATION OF WORD PAIRS

1. (M) big—bag ____
2. (E) lease—leash ____
3. (S) pot—pot ____
4. (B) latch—patch ____
5. (S) bus—bus ____
6. (M) fest—fast ____
7. (E) muff—muss ____
8. (S) tiger—tiger ____
9. (M) rope—rap ____
10. (B) glad—dad ____
11. (M) noon—none ____
12. (E) cat—cap ____
13. (B) fun—run ____
14. (S) man—man ____
15. (B) shack—lack ____

16. (M) lip—lap ____
17. (E) dim—din ____
18. (S) king—king ____
19. (B) dump—lump ____
20. (S) live—live ____
21. (E) much—mush ____
22. (M) ton—ten ____
23. (B) chair—pair ____
24. (E) mouth—mouse ____
25. (M) pet—pat ____
26. (E) sheaf—sheath ____
27. (S) fed—fed ____
28. (B) tug—lug ____
29. (M) led—lad ____
30. (B) past—last ____

Word pair differences:

8 middle

7 ending

8 beginning

Word pairs the same: 7

PRELITERACY AND EMERGING LITERACY ASSESSMENT

This section is designed to ascertain strengths and weaknesses of students who are unable to read the graded word lists or passages. The tests are provided to give the examiner specific information regarding preliteracy and emerging literacy skills. Included are tests to diagnose the metalinguistic skills of literacy awareness and phonemic manipulation. *Literacy awareness* deals with the student's ability to understand concepts related to reading, while *manipulation* refers to one's ability to both isolate and blend segments of language.

Letter knowledge is divided into the areas of recognition, identification, and reproduction. A student is able to recognize a letter when, from a given list, he or she can select one that has been named by the examiner. This task is easier than letter identification, which requires the student to name the letter. If a student can identify the letters, then it is unnecessary to administer the letter recognition test, since it is a prerequisite skill. However, for remediation purposes, it is helpful to ascertain if the student recognizes any unidentified letters. Of the three areas, letter reproduction is the most difficult. Students may show strengths and weaknesses in all three areas depending on the given letters. For example, an individual may be able to reproduce certain letters but only recognize or identify others.

Oral language and early print awareness are assessed with syntax matching tests and semantic and syntactic cloze tests. Spelling test 1 may be given to assess phonemic manipulation through invented spelling. Finally, visual discrimination and auditory discrimination tests are presented to rule out disabilities in these areas.

A testing record is provided on p. 111.

LITERACY AWARENESS:
ASSESSMENT OF BEGINNING CONCEPTS ABOUT PRINT

ADMINISTRATION: The following Literacy Concepts interviews require a child's book, paper, and markers or pencil.

INTERPRETATION: Record acquired and unacquired concepts for use in remediation. These concepts are best developed over time by incorporating explanations into literacy lessons.

LITERACY CONCEPTS—INTERVIEW I

DIRECTIONS: Write *A* for Acceptable or *NA* for Not Acceptable in the blank.

1. Hand the child the book so that it is upside down and backward from his or her point of view. Say, *"Let's look at this book."* Observe whether the child turns the book upright. If the child does not spontaneously turn the book over and open it at the beginning, say, *"Where does this book start?"*

    Child turns book upright _____

    Child correctly identifies beginning of book _____

2. Ask the child to tell you what is happening in the book. If the child is unable or unwilling to do so, offer to read the book.

    Child produces a plausible narrative _____

3. After the child has narrated a few pages (or the examiner has read a few pages), pause and ask the child, *"Where does it say that?"*

    Child points to printed text _____

4. If the child successfully points to printed text, ask him or her to point to a word.

    Child points to a single word _____

5. Give the child a clean sheet of paper and a selection of colored markers and pencils. Ask him or her to *"draw something."* When the child has completed the drawing, or after a few minutes, remove the first paper, give the child another clean sheet of paper and ask him or her to write something. Record the child's comments during each activity. Note whether the child's intent appears to be appropriate to each task (e.g., when writing). Look for evidence of distinction between drawing and writing in the finished products (e.g., linear forms for writing vs. circular forms for drawing, or vice versa).

    Child distinguishes between drawing and writing _____

LITERACY CONCEPTS—INTERVIEW II

DIRECTIONS: Write *A* for Acceptable or *NA* for Not Acceptable in the blank.

A/NA	Concept	Directions
_____	page	Say, *"Please turn the page"* or *"Name the picture on any page."*
_____	letter	Say, *"Can you point to any letter on this page?"* or write down three symbols (& % B) and say: *"Pick the one that's a letter."*
_____	word	Write three words in a row and say, *"Circle any word."* (e.g., *How are you?*)
_____	line	Say, *"Point to any line on the page, run your finger until the line is finished."*
_____	first/last/middle	Say, *"Point to the first and last word on the page."* Show three words and say, *"Point to the first word." "Point to the second word." "Point to the last word."*
_____	before/after	Indicate any word on the page. Say, *"I have my finger on this word. You point to the word before this word." "Point to the word after this word."* (If not known, use three physical objects.)
_____	top/bottom	Say, *"Look at this page. Point to the top of the page. Point to the bottom of the page."* (If not known, use a glass.)
_____	above	Point to a line in the middle of the page. Say, *"Look at the line where my finger is. Point to the line above. Point to the line below."* (If not known, use a physical object.)
_____	sentence	Read a short paragraph to the child. Before beginning, say, *"I am going to read to you some sentences. When I have finished the first one, hold up your hand."*

PHONEMIC MANIPULATION

The reader's ability to both *blend* sounds together to produce a word and *segment* a word into phonemes (sounds) are metalinguistic skills that contribute to decoding.

Blending

Blending includes responding to a sequence of isolated speech sounds by recognizing the phonemes and pronouncing the word they constitute.

When testing the child's ability to blend, do not show the child the written material. The child hears the individual sounds and then tries to blend them together.

DIRECTIONS: Say, "*I am going to say some sounds that when put together make up a whole word. Listen to the individual sounds and then tell me the word the sounds would make when put together. Let's do one together.*" Write the student's response.

Sample: *D/I/SH makes what word?* (dish)

Say, "*Now let's do a few more.*"

Segmenting

Segmenting requires the child to discriminate the phonemes within a word and pronounce them in the correct sequence.

The child sees no written material. This skill is the reverse of blending; the child hears the word and then pronounces the phonemes or syllables separately.

DIRECTIONS: Say, "*I am going to say a word; then you say the sounds or word parts that make up that word. Let's do one together. In the word dog, the word parts are D/O/G/. Let's do a few more. I'll give you the word, and you give me the word parts.*" Write the sounds the student says.

INTERPRETATION: As children and adults learn to read and write, they usually attend to the first phoneme in a word, then the last phoneme, and finally the middle sounds (see Table 2 on p. 80). Compare the student responses here with the test results of the Hearing Letter Names in the Words Test, the Spelling Tests, and the Auditory Discrimination Test.

BLENDING

	Word Parts	Word	Response
1.	F / EE / D	feed	_____
2.	M / A / N	man	_____
3.	D / AY	day	_____
4.	S / PI / DER	spider	_____
5.	PO / TA / TO	potato	_____

SEGMENTATION

	Word	Word Parts	Response
1.	cat	C / A / T	_____
2.	bed	B / E / D	_____
3.	soap	S / OA / P	_____
4.	time	T / I / M / E	_____
5.	face	F / A / CE	_____

LETTER KNOWLEDGE

Letter Recognition

The examiner says a letter and the student points to it. This is a prerequisite skill to letter identification and would only be given if the student were unable to identify the letter.

DIRECTIONS: Say, *"When I name a letter, point to it."* Record all letters not known. Record all letters called in error. Look for confusion of letters: *m/n, u/n, p/b,* and *d/q.*

Letter Identification

The examiner points to a letter and the student says its name.

DIRECTIONS: Say, *"Name these letters in line one, two. . . ."* Record all letters not known. Record all letters called in error. Look for confusion of letters: *m/n, u/n, p/b,* and *d/q.*

Letter Writing

The student is required to write down either capital or lowercase letters of the alphabet.

DIRECTIONS: Say, *"When I name a letter, write it on the paper."* Record all letters not known. Record all letters called in error. Indicate letters recognized (R), identified (I), written (W).

Uppercase	*Known*	*Not Known*	*Lowercase*	*Known*	*Not Known*
B	____	____	m	____	____
C	____	____	y	____	____
D	____	____	n	____	____
S	____	____	l	____	____
A	____	____	r	____	____
I	____	____	o	____	____
F	____	____	t	____	____
E	____	____	p	____	____
M	____	____	z	____	____
L	____	____	v	____	____
P	____	____	k	____	____
T	____	____	i	____	____
R	____	____	a	____	____
Z	____	____	j	____	____
J	____	____	u	____	____
W	____	____	g	____	____
X	____	____	w	____	____
G	____	____	b	____	____
U	____	____	c	____	____
H	____	____	s	____	____
Q	____	____	h	____	____
K	____	____	d	____	____
N	____	____	f	____	____
Y	____	____	x	____	____
V	____	____	q	____	____
O	____	____	e	____	____

Able to recite alphabet: _____ Yes _____ No   Comments: _____

LETTER KNOWLEDGE

Uppercase

B C D S A I F E M L P T R

Z J W X G U H Q K N Y V O

Lowercase

m y n l r o t p z v k i a

j u g w b c s h d f x q e

HEARING LETTER NAMES IN WORDS

Those students who know the names of letters can be tested for the ability to hear letter names in words in order to assess a basic area of phonemic discrimination and segmentation useful in beginning reading.

ADMINISTRATION: Say, *"Listen to this word to see if you can hear letter names in words. Zebra. Say zebra. What is the first letter heard in zebra?"* Give the following list of words in the same way.

INTERPRETATION: Correct identification of at least eight letter names indicates the ability to use letter names as a clue to word recognition.

1. open
2. beach
3. acorn
4. Jason
5. X-ray
6. peek
7. ice
8. deep
9. Kate
10. unicorn
11. team
12. each

HEARING LETTER NAMES IN WORDS

_____ o	1.	open
_____ b	2.	beach
_____ a	3.	acorn
_____ j	4.	Jason
_____ x	5.	X-ray
_____ p	6.	peek
_____ i	7.	ice
_____ d	8.	deep
_____ k	9.	Kate
_____ u	10.	unicorn
_____ t	11.	team
_____ e	12.	each

SYNTAX MATCHING

This task may be used with nonreaders. It tests the ability of the student to recognize words as separate speech entities that can be recorded in print.

ADMINISTRATION: Place the test in front of the child. Put another sheet of paper or a card under the first example. Say, *"This says,* **Go home.** *Say,* **Go home.** *Say it again. Now point to the word that says Go."* If necessary, point to each word separately and say, *"**Go . . . home.** This word is* **go.**" Then do the next example. Say, *"This says,* **Look out.** *Say,* **Look out.** *Say it again. Point to the word that says* **out.**" Demonstrate as necessary. Use the following procedure with the six test sentences.

Syntax Matching Test

This says:	You say it.	Say it again.	Point to:
Close the door.	″	″	close
Pet the dog.	″	″	dog
See his new hat.	″	″	new
Her puppy is barking.	″	″	barking
This horse can run fast.	″	″	run
You can go with me.	″	″	with

Number correct _____

INTERPRETATION: A score of at least four correct words can serve as one indication that the child is aware of separate words in sentences and that these can be printed sequentially. Discount the score if the child appears to be guessing. Since this is a brief sample of one ability, other indications of reading readiness, such as naming and writing letters, should be considered.

SYNTAX MATCHING TEST

Example A	Go home.

Example B	Look out.

1.	Close the door.

2.	Pet the dog.

3.	See his new hat.

4.	Her puppy is barking.

5.	This horse can run fast.

6.	You can go with me.

SEMANTIC AND SYNTACTIC EVALUATION: CLOZE TESTS

Cloze tests may be given to determine if students are able to use semantic and syntactic cues as aids to comprehension and word identification. Students use semantic cues if their previous experiences and meaning vocabulary enable them to predict an upcoming word in a sentence. For example, in the sentence

When the tire blew, the car immediately veered toward the side of the road.

a reader may substitute for *car* any of the words *auto, motor car, vehicle, sedan, jalopy,* or *lemon* and still retain the general meaning. This type of substitution indicates that the reader uses semantic cues.

Syntactic cues are based on the syntax of the sentence. In order to use these, a reader must have a developed language structure. If in the example the reader read *dog* for car, he or she would be using syntactic cues because he or she substituted one noun for another. While readers generally use both cue systems concurrently, it is helpful to determine the extent to which each is emphasized.

Included in the next section are four cloze subtests. Cloze I (Cloze Test for Beginning Readers) is intended for those students reading from primer through second-grade levels and examines their abilities to use context as an aid to word identification and comprehension. Cloze II (Semantic Cloze Test) may be given to children ranging from nonreaders to those reading on a primary level and is designed to measure the child's level of cultural experiences as well as language development, association, retrieval, and expression. Cloze III (Syntactic Cloze Test) is recommended for students reading at or above the second-grade level and measures the reader's sentence structure development and ability to use syntax in making predictions. Cloze IV (Grammatical Closure) is designed to assess mastery of grammatical forms for language-delayed students.

CLOZE TEST FOR BEGINNING READERS (CLOZE I)

PURPOSE AND LEVEL: This supplementary test may be given to students reading on primer through second-grade levels to examine their abilities to use context as an aid to comprehension.

ADMINISTRATION: If capable, the student should read the sentence. However, if he or she is unable to do so, the examiner may read while the child listens. Have the child point to the words as they are read.

INSTRUCTIONS: Say, "*This story has some words missing. Try to read the story by guessing the missing words.*" If the child is unable to read the passage, say, "*I will read each line of the story. You point to each word I say. Try to guess the missing word.*" Repeat lines as necessary.

SCORING AND INTERPRETATION: Any word that is semantically and syntactically suitable is acceptable; however, it must be suitable in the context of the entire paragraph. For example, if sentence six (But they do not _____ too much.) is taken out of context, such words as *eat, drive,* and *play* would be acceptable. Within the context of the entire paragraph, however, they would be incorrect semantically. The following are some possible correct answers. The examiner may determine that other substitutions are both semantically and syntactically correct as well.

1. The rain came down all _____ . (*day, night, evening*)
2. We could not go _____ . (*out, outside*)
3. We wanted the rain to _____ . (*stop, slow down*)
4. _____ makes plants grow. (*Rain, Water*)
5. Farmers _____ the rain. (*want, need*)
6. But they do not _____ too much. (*need, want, desire*)
7. Too much _____ can kill the (*rain, water*)
8. _____ (*crops, potatoes*)

Answer Sheet—Responses

	Semantically		Syntactically	
	acceptable	*not acceptable*	*acceptable*	*not acceptable*
1.	____	____	____	____
2.	____	____	____	____
3.	____	____	____	____
4.	____	____	____	____
5.	____	____	____	____
6.	____	____	____	____
7.	____	____	____	____
8.	____	____	____	____

Students should be able to guess at least five words out of eight. Students who have unusual difficulty in pointing to words as the sentences are read aloud may not have developed an appropriate concept of a word.

1. The rain came down all _____ .

2. We could not go _____ .

3. We wanted the rain to _____ .

4. _____ makes plants grow.

5. Farmers _____ the rain.

6. But they do not _____ too much.

7. Too much _____ can kill the

8. _____ .

SEMANTIC CLOZE TEST (CLOZE II)

PURPOSE AND LEVEL: This test may be given to nonreaders or those on a primary level. It contains ten sentences that students should be able to complete based on their background of experiences. Those who have difficulty may not have had the cultural experiences implicit in the sentences, or they may have problems in language development, association, retrieval, or expression.

ADMINISTRATION: The examiner reads the sentences to the student. If she or he is unable to respond, supply the correct answer and then proceed with the next sentence. Stop if the student misses three.

INSTRUCTIONS: Say, "*I will read some sentences with the last word missing. Try to guess the missing word. Let's do one for practice. 'He jumped up and _____ .' *" If the student does not respond appropriately, say, "*Down. He jumped up and down. Let's try this one.*"

SCORING AND INTERPRETATION: Accept reasonable guesses. Children between six and eight should miss no more than five. Older students should miss no more than three.

Discuss missed items that may reflect a lack of experience. If experiential background is ruled out as a source of inability to respond, further evaluation of language facility may be indicated.

Since shyness, hostility, or refusal to cooperate may be a factor, other observations should be made before referring the student.

The following are some possible correct answers. The examiner may determine that other substitutions are semantically and syntactically correct as well.

1. door, window, drawer
2. brother
3. hot
4. hospital
5. change
6. mat, rug
7. drawer
8. cool, cold
9. cry, scream
10. race, game, contest

SEMANTIC CLOZE TEST (CLOZE II)

1. Please close the _____ .

2. She has one sister and one _____ .

3. I burned my tongue because the soup was _____ .

4. He hurt his leg and went to the emergency room at the _____ .

5. I waited at the crosswalk for the light to _____ .

6. Please wipe your feet on the _____ .

7. Put your clothes in the dresser _____ .

8. She put on a coat because she was _____ .

9. A loud noise made the baby _____ .

10. The team was happy because they won the _____ .

SYNTACTIC CLOZE TEST (CLOZE III)

PURPOSE AND LEVEL: This test is more difficult than Cloze II and is recommended for students reading at or above the second-grade level. The purpose is to determine which sentence parts the student finds difficult. This test contains ten sentences that require the student to guess a missing word that is both semantically and syntactically correct.

ADMINISTRATION: The student reads each sentence, first silently, then orally, supplying the missing word.

INSTRUCTIONS: Say, *"These sentences have some words missing. Try to guess what they are. Read each sentence to yourself, then read it to me."*

SCORING AND INTERPRETATION: Accept reasonable guesses that fit the meaning and the part of speech required. Make a record of sentence parts that are difficult for the student.

1. He waited for his _____ .   (*noun*)
2. Your new shirt is _____ .   (*adjective*)
3. I can't _____ very fast.   (*verb*)
4. She gave _____ mother some flowers.   (*pronoun*)
5. I like hotdogs, _____ I like hamburgers better.   (*conjunction*)
6. Talk _____ so they can't hear you.   (*adverb*)
7. Put the cup _____ the table.   (*preposition*)
8. They like baseball _____ football.   (*conjunction*)
9. The dog _____ barking.   (*verb*)
10. He came here _____ another city.   (*preposition*)

SYNTACTIC CLOZE TEST (CLOZE III)

1. He waited for his _____ .

2. Your new shirt is _____ .

3. I can't _____ very fast.

4. She gave _____ mother some flowers.

5. I like hotdogs, _____ I like hamburgers better.

6. Talk _____ so they can't hear you.

7. Put the cup _____ the table.

8. They like baseball _____ football.

9. The dog _____ barking.

10. He came here _____ another city.

GRAMMATICAL CLOSURE (CLOZE IV)

PURPOSE AND LEVEL: The grammatical closure test may be given to students whose speech seems to be inadequately developed. This may be the result of delayed language. Students learning English as a second language may be given the inventory to learn which forms may need to be reviewed and practiced.

ADMINISTRATION: The examiner reads the sentences to the student. If the student misses the first sentence, give the correct response, and practice with similar constructions until the task is understood. Demonstrate with pencils, books, and other objects when necessary.

INSTRUCTIONS: Say, "*I am going to read some sentences to you that have some words missing. Try to guess the missing word.*"

SCORING AND INTERPRETATION: Accept responses that fit the grammatical form, such as *pens* for *pencils* in sentence 1, and *mine* for *yours* in sentence 2. Repeat with appropriate demonstration if the student gives a response such as *shoes* for *feet* in sentence 10. Make a record of grammatical forms that need to be taught. Since this test is quite short, other samples of the student's language may need to be obtained. The recommended procedure is to tape a sample of about 200 words, transcribe the sample, and categorize the forms with which the student is having difficulty. Compare the student's language competency with his or her peers. Refer to a speech therapist if the problems seem to be severe.

GRAMMATICAL CLOSURE (CLOZE IV)

1. This is a pencil. Here are two _____. (*plural*)

2. This is my pencil. That pencil is _____. (*possessive pronoun*)

3. I can tap my pencil. Now I am _____. (*present participle*)

4. I saw one man. Then I saw three _____. (*plural*)

5. The child breaks his toys. Now all of the toys have been _____. (*past participle*)

6. This book belongs to Nancy. Whose book is it? It is _____. (*possessive*)

7. I have a box and you have a box. We have two _____. (*plural*)

8. This book is on the table. Where is this book? (*demonstrate over or under*)

   _____ the table. (*preposition*)

9. This book is big. This one is bigger. And this one is the _____. (*comparative adjective*)

10. This is a foot. Here are two _____. (*plural*)

11. He said he would go; now he has _____. (*past participle*)

12. She was writing. Look at what she has _____. (*past participle*)

13. Mary has many pencils, but Sue has even _____. (*comparative adjective*)

14. I saw a mouse; then I saw two _____. (*plural*)

15. Tim enjoyed himself at the party. Tina enjoyed herself. They both enjoyed

    _____. (*plural possessive*)

PRELITERACY ASSESSMENT
TESTING RECORD

Testing Record	Unsatisfactory	Satisfactory	Specific Problem Area
1. Literacy Concepts			
2. Phonemic Manipulation:			
Blending			
Segmenting			
3. Letter Knowledge:			
a. Recognition			
b. Identification			
c. Reproduction			
4. Hearing Letter Names in Words			
5. Syntax Matching			
6. Cloze Tests:			
Beginning Reading			
Semantic			
Syntactic			
Grammatical			
7. Visual Discrimination			
8. Auditory Discrimination			
9. Spelling, Test 1			

PHONICS AND STRUCTURAL ANALYSIS TEST

Contents of the Test

Phonics	Structural Analysis
1. Initial Single Consonants	8. Inflectional Suffixes
2. Consonant Blends	9. Derivational Suffixes
3. Consonant Digraphs	10. Prefixes
4. Short Vowel Sounds	11. Compound Words
5. Long Vowel Sounds	
6. Vowel Digraphs	
7. Reversals	

PHONICS TEST

Information about a student's knowledge of sound-symbol association, ability to blend sounds, and knowledge of structural analysis can be obtained by administering a Phonics Test and Analysis. The subtests in this section have been designed to determine if students know grapheme-phoneme correspondence of phonetically regular elements. Nonsense words are used to ensure that the student is not simply pronouncing words by sight. The results of this test should be compared with the student's ability to read words in context so that a qualitative analysis can be made with regard to the student's application of his or her graphemic, syntactic, and semantic knowledge.

ADMINISTRATION: Select only those subtests that appear to be appropriate. For example, a student who can read second-grade-level passages probably should not be given the subtest on consonant sounds, and a student whose highest instructional level is first grade should not be given the syllabication subtest.

Introduce each test by reading the directions on the subtest page. Mark responses on the examiner's copy accompanying each subtest. Record the student's responses by putting a line through those that are correct and writing incorrect responses above the missed elements. Circle elements not attempted. The Testing Record on p. 126 is helpful for summarization purposes.

INTERPRETATION: Most readers apply their background of experiences and knowledge of language so that they make use of context to predict the content words in a passage. Generally, the first one or two letters of a word, along with syntactic and semantic context, are used in word recognition. When necessary, the reader resorts to an analysis of the entire word and confirms his or her results with the context. One purpose of the Phonics and Word Analysis Test is to learn whether the reader has the knowledge and ability to analyze words not immediately recognized. A record can be kept of sound-symbol associations that have not been acquired, ability to blend sounds, and structural analysis abilities so that sufficient assistance can be given in these areas to enable the reader to recognize words in context. *Caution:* Some readers have great difficulty in phonetic analysis and should not be drilled in this skill. Other readers will be overly analytic in their application of phonetic and structural analysis. They will need to learn to read for meaning. These situations indicate the need for the diagnostician to put word analysis in the proper perspective.

PHONICS TEST

Initial Single Consonants, Consonant Blends, and Consonant Digraphs

INSTRUCTIONS: Say, *"Look at the two letters in the middle (shaded) column.* **OP** *is pronounced /op/. Name the letter(s) in the first column, pronounce the* **op** *in the middle column, and then say the nonsense word in the third column by adding the first letter(s) to the middle word."*

If necessary, tell the student the *op* sound, because the purpose in giving these subtests is to determine knowledge of the initial letter(s). The student should not have difficulty blending the initial sound with the *op*. Make certain the student can pronounce *op* before the test begins. When the student can identify the sound of /op/, continue with the test.

Record all responses on the Answer Sheet (below). Indicate any incorrect sounds substituted by the student.

Consonants, blends, and digraphs are usually introduced in the first and second grades.

Answer Sheet

Initial Single Consonants

1. b	7. j	13. r
2. c	8. k	14. s
3. d	9. l	15. t
4. f	10. m	16. v
5. g	11. n	17. w
6. h	12. p	18. z

Consonant Blends

1. bl	9. gr	17. sp
2. br	10. pl	18. st
3. cl	11. pr	19. sw
4. cr	12. sc	20. tr
5. dr	13. sk	21. tw
6. fr	14. sl	22. scr
7. fl	15. sm	23. str
8. gl	16. sn	

Consonant Digraphs

1. sh
2. ch
3. ph
4. th
5. wh

PHONICS TEST

Initial Single Consonants
op

1. b	op	bop
2. c	op	cop
3. d	op	dop
4. f	op	fop
5. g	op	gop
6. h	op	hop
7. j	op	jop
8. k	op	kop
9. l	op	lop

10. m	op	mop
11. n	op	nop
12. p	op	pop
13. r	op	rop
14. s	op	sop
15. t	op	top
16. v	op	vop
17. w	op	wop
18. z	op	zop

PHONICS TEST

Consonant Blends
op

1.	bl	op	blop
2.	br	op	brop
3.	cl	op	clop
4.	cr	op	crop
5.	dr	op	drop
6.	fr	op	frop
7.	fl	op	flop
8.	gl	op	glop
9.	gr	op	grop
10.	pl	op	plop
11.	pr	op	prop

12.	sc	op	scop
13.	sk	op	skop
14.	sl	op	slop
15.	sm	op	smop
16.	sn	op	snop
17.	sp	op	spop
18.	st	op	stop
19.	sw	op	swop
20.	tr	op	trop
21.	tw	op	twop
22.	scr	op	scrop
23.	str	op	strop

PHONICS TEST

Consonant Digraphs
op

1.	sh	op	shop
2.	ch	op	chop
3.	ph	op	phop
4.	th	op	thop
5.	wh	op	whop

PHONICS TEST

Short Vowels, Long Vowels, and Vowel Digraphs

INSTRUCTIONS: Nonsense words are used when testing for knowledge of grapheme-phoneme relationships to ensure the word is not known by sight. Say, *"Look at the letter(s) in the first column; then pronounce the nonsense or silly word beside it."*

Record the answer on the Answer Sheet (below) by indicating incorrect responses.

Short and long vowel sounds are usually introduced in first grade, and vowel digraphs in the second and third grades.

Answer Sheet

Short Vowel Sounds	*Long Vowels—Silent E Ending*
1. a	6. i
2. i	7. o
3. e	8. e
4. o	9. u
5. u	10. a

Long Vowels—Double Vowel Combinations

11. oa
12. ea
13. ai
14. ee

Vowel Digraphs

15. oo (as in *loose, food*)	20. oi (as in *oil*)
16. oo (as in *cook, stood*)	21. oy (as in *boy*)
17. ew (as in *few, stew*)	22. ou (as in *out*)
18. au (as in *author*)	23. ow (as in *cow*)
19. aw (as in *straw*)	24. ow (as in *mow*)

PHONICS TEST

Short Vowel Sounds

1. a fap
2. i fip
3. e fep
4. o fop
5. u fup

Long Vowels—Silent *E* Ending

6. i fite
7. o fote
8. e fete
9. u fute
10. a fate

Long Vowels—Double Vowel Combinations

11. oa oam
12. ea eam
13. ai aim
14. ee eem

PHONICS TEST

Vowel Digraphs

15. oo—tood

16. oo—sook

17. ew—tew

       lew

18. au—aut

       aup

19. aw—awf

       awp

       faw

20. oi—oip

       oit

       loi

21. oy—roy

       moy

       foy

22. ou—ouf

23. ow—cow

24. ow—tow

PHONICS TEST

Reversals

INSTRUCTIONS: Say, *"Read these words as fast as you can."*
A student who retains the early tendency of some children to reverse words—*saw* for *was, on* for *no,* and so on—
will usually slip if he reads the test words rapidly. It is not unusual for children to make reversals until the third grade
level.

Answer Sheet

	Correct	*Incorrect*
1. pal	_____	_____
2. no	_____	_____
3. saw	_____	_____
4. raw	_____	_____
5. ten	_____	_____
6. tar	_____	_____
7. won	_____	_____
8. pot	_____	_____
9. was	_____	_____
10. on	_____	_____
11. lap	_____	_____
12. tops	_____	_____

PHONICS TEST

Reversals

pal

no

saw

raw

ten

tar

won

pot

was

on

lap

tops

STRUCTURAL ANALYSIS

Inflectional and Derivational Suffixes and Prefixes

INFLECTIONAL SUFFIXES: Suffixes are usually taught before prefixes and should be added to a word already known by sight. Inflectional suffixes (*s, ed, ing, er, est, ier, y*) are placed at the end of a root word for grammatical purposes. They are usually introduced during the latter half of the first grade. This marks the beginning of structural analysis instruction. Children who are able to identify words with inflectional suffixes may then undertake the more complicated task of learning derivational suffixes. If students have difficulty with inflectional suffixes, show them a learned base word and add the suffix to be taught. Present the student with enough examples to clarify the concept.

play	*work*	*jump*
played	*worked*	*jumped*

DERIVATIONAL SUFFIXES: Derivational suffixes are generally introduced in the second and third grades. Children should be able to see and pronounce the suffix as one unit. Carefully note the specific suffix(es) with which the student has difficulty. Remediation of derivational suffixes is best accomplished through inductive (discovery) teaching. Select the suffix to be taught (e.g., *less*), and add it to several root words the child already knows.

mother	*home*	*tooth*
motherless	*homeless*	*toothless*

Finally, present the student with additional words containing the suffix to determine if the skill has been transferred.

PREFIXES: Prefixes are generally introduced in the second grade after inflectional suffixes and the most common derivational suffixes. Remediate unknown prefixes using the same procedure recommended for derivational suffixes. Select the prefix(es) to be taught, based on the test results. Add the prefix to several known words.

happy	*fair*	*pleasant*
unhappy	*unfair*	*unpleasant*

Have the student note how the prefix affects the root word. Give additional words for practice.

STRUCTURAL ANALYSIS

Inflectional and Derivational Suffixes and Prefixes

INSTRUCTIONS: Nonsense words are used when testing for knowledge of prefixes and suffixes to ensure that the words are not known by sight. Say, *"Read these nonsense words as well as you can."* Carefully note the specific suffixes and prefixes with which the student experiences difficulty. Mark correct and incorrect responses on the Answer Sheet (below).

Answer Sheet

Inflectional Suffixes	*Prefixes*	
1. s	1. mono	28. mis
2. ed	2. photo	29. co
3. ing	3. poly	30. anti
4. er	4. auto	31. semi
5. est	5. sub	32. trans
6. ly	6. un	
7. ier	7. dis	
	8. in	
Derivational Suffixes	9. pre	
8. ness	10. be	
9. ment	11. non	
10. tion	12. fore	
11. less	13. counter	
12. ful	14. under	
13. ar	15. super	
14. ic	16. tele	
15. ence	17. therm	
16. ship	18. post	
17. age	19. mini	
18. ous	20. photo	
19. ive	21. bi	
20. ant	22. pro	
21. ance	23. en	
22. able	24. ex	
23. hood	25. re	
24. wood	26. con	
	27. de	

STRUCTURAL ANALYSIS

Inflectional Suffixes

1. flays

2. flayed

3. flaying

4. flayer

5. flayest

6. flayly

7. flaier

Derivational Suffixes

8. bookness

9. carment

10. hilltion

11. drumless

12. bandful

13. lugar

14. felic

15. tendence

16. bendship

17. fileage

18. tubous

19. bandive

20. burnant

21. pondance

22. fourable

23. mildhood

24. bestwood

STRUCTURAL ANALYSIS

Prefixes

1. monotell
2. phototop
3. polygon
4. autogo
5. subman
6. ungo
7. distap
8. inwell
9. prehit
10. besell
11. nongo
12. forehit
13. counterhid
14. undertap
15. supercap
16. telecot

17. thermtop
18. postless
19. minigo
20. photohid
21. biwin
22. prohid
23. enrun
24. exwin
25. recar
26. conmet
27. depan
28. mislead
29. codial
30. antirun
31. semidid
32. transcon

STRUCTURAL ANALYSIS

Compound Words

INSTRUCTIONS: Say, "*Read these words as well as you can.*" If the student misses these words, try a trial teaching sequence. Cover the second part of a word and ask for pronunciation of the first part; then cover the first part and ask for pronunciation; finally, uncover the entire word and ask for pronunciation. Ask the student to do the next one independently.

stairway

workhorse

mealtime

carwash

railroad

nightbank

houseboat

headstrong

firehouse

withdrew

outrage

sagebrush

stovepipe

overturned

lollypop

paperjumper

basketmeet

storyteller

screwdriver

dealership

understood

STRUCTURAL ANALYSIS

Compound Words

stairway

workhorse

mealtime

carwash

railroad

nightbank

houseboat

headstrong

firehouse

withdrew

outrage

sagebrush

stovepipe

overturned

lollypop

paperjumper

basketmeet

storyteller

screwdriver

dealership

understood

PHONICS TEST AND STRUCTURAL ANALYSIS

Testing Record

Phonics

1. *Initial Single Consonants*

   b   c   d   f   g   h   j   k   l   m   n   p   r   s   t   v   w   z

2. *Consonant Blends*

   bl   br   cl   cr   dr   fr   fl   gl   gr   pl   pr   sc   sk   sl

   sm   sn   sp   st   sw   tr   tw   scr   str

3. *Consonant Digraphs*

   sh   ch   ph   th   wh

4. *Short Vowels*

   a   i   e   o   u

5. *Long Vowels—Silent E Ending*   *Double Vowel Combinations*

   i   o   e   u   a   oa   ea   ai   ee

6. *Vowel Digraphs*

   oo   (as in *loose, food*)   oo   (as in *cook, stood*)   ew   (as in *few, stew*)   au   (as in *author*)

   aw   (as in *straw*)   oi   (as in *oil*)   oy   (as in *boy*)   ou   (as in *out*)

   ow   (as in *cow*)   ow   (as in *mow*)

7. *Reversals*

   pal   no   saw   raw   ten   tar

   won   pot   was   on   lap   tops

Structural Analysis

8. *Inflectional Suffixes*

   s   ed   ing   er   est   ly   ier

9. *Derivational Suffixes*

   ness   ment   tion   less   ful   ar   ic   ence   ship

   age   ous   ive   ant   ance   able   hood   wood

10. *Prefixes*

    mono   photo   poly   auto   sub   un   dis   in   pre   be   non

    fore   counter   under   super   tele   therm   post   mini   photo

    bi   pro   en   ex   re   con   de   mis   co   anti   semi   trans

11. *Compound Words*

    stairway   workhorse   mealtime   carwash

    railroad   nightbank   houseboat   headstrong

    firehouse   withdrew   outrage   sagebrush

    stovepipe   overturned   lollypop   paperjumper

    basketmeet   storyteller   screwdriver   dealership   understood

ORAL LANGUAGE

EVALUATION OF EXPRESSION

Several methods may be employed to elicit oral language. The strategy or strategies used will depend on which aspects of language need to be evaluated and the degree of development. The following procedures are recommended.

1. Describing

Show the student a picture suitable to her or his maturity, with three or more actors (people or animals) engaged in easily recognized activities. Say, *"Please look at the picture and tell me as much as you can about it."* As necessary, encourage the student to continue. Say, *"Good, tell me some more,"* and *"Fine, go on."* If at all possible, tape the student; then transcribe the tape. If a tape can't be made, write the student's utterances. A show-and-tell activity might be used if the student is not intimidated by being in front of a group. Analyze the speech sample, and record the results on the Oral Language Expression Checklist (p. 130).

2. Retelling

Read to the student a passage of 60 to 100 words, suitable in length and content to the student's maturity and interest. The passage should have a well-organized content. Ask the student to retell the story. Tape, transcribe, and analyze the performance as outlined in procedure 1 and record results on the checklist. (Retelling information may also be obtained from the highest independent-level performance on graded passages.)

3. Dictating

Have the student make up a story and dictate it to the examiner. Pictures or opening sentences (story starters) may be used to stimulate the student. Analyze and record the results on the Oral Language Expression Checklist (p. 130).

ORAL LANGUAGE EXPRESSION CHECKLIST

Yes	No	Comparison with Peers Indicates Satisfactory Performance in:	Description and Examples of Problems
____	____	Articulation	
____	____	English as a second language	
____	____	Fluency	
____	____	Volume	
____	____	Voice quality	
____	____	Other speech areas	

Vocabulary Development

Yes	No		
____	____	Understanding of connotation	
____	____	Definition by use (*chair*—sit on it)	
____	____	Definition by description (has four legs)	
____	____	Definition by category (furniture)	

Level of Abstraction

Yes	No		
____	____	Description of action or quality	
____	____	Interpretation of actions or events	
____	____	Prediction of actions or events	
____	____	Evaluation of actions or events	

Syntactic Development

Yes	No		
____	____	Use of simple sentences (subject-verb)	
____	____	Use of compound subjects or verbs	
____	____	Use of compound sentences	
____	____	Use of passive voice	
____	____	Use of subordinate conjunctions	
____	____	Use of sentences with more than one dependent clause	
____	____	Sentence length	
____	____	Grammar	
____	____	Ability to repeat sentences	

Organization of Expression

Yes	No		
____	____	Appropriateness	
____	____	Coherence	
____	____	Organized retelling of narrative: main characters, problem, events, sequence. If important, causality, outcome, and generalizations, moral or theme.	
____	____	Organized retelling of nonfiction: purpose, main points, order, cause and effect, comparison or contrast, conclusion	
____	____	Telling a story (as above)	
____	____	Explaining, describing, informing (as above)	

EVALUATION OF ORAL LANGUAGE RECEPTION

Some students may have difficulty in oral language expression yet do well in language reception. Others may be weak in both areas. Generally, receptive language comprehension is more advanced than expressive language. The listening comprehension section of the Graded Passages test can be used as one measure of oral language reception. Other informal assessment procedures for those with poor listening comprehension include giving directions to which the student responds physically. For example: "*Put this book on the table.*" Oral commissions may be given in increasing levels of difficulty in terms of abstractness, number, and sequence of commands. *Put this book on the table* is concrete and consists of one command. *Point to the largest book* is more abstract. *Put the book on the table; next, turn off the lamp, and then bring me an eraser* is a command with three sequenced parts. How well a student performs is an indication of her or his ability to comprehend spoken language. Following directions is difficult for those with receptive language problems. It may be useful to contrast the student's abilities in nonverbal areas such as drawing, painting, crafts, and similar activities with verbal performance. Also, arithmetic calculation abilities can be contrasted with arithmetic reasoning in story problems.

Some of the testing procedures listed under Oral Language and Cloze Tests may be used to evaluate receptive language abilities, but one should keep in mind that most require oral responses. Those who appear to have difficulties in oral language reception should be referred to specialists in communication disorders for more careful evaluation and, if necessary, language development. Of course, the need for an auditory acuity evaluation is also indicated to rule out hearing difficulties.

The Peabody Picture Vocabulary Test (revised 1981; Circle Pines, MN: American Guidance Service) may be quite useful in evaluating oral language reception. The examiner should consider the student's background of experience and the demands of the test to determine whether it is appropriate.

WRITING

EVALUATION

Handwriting: Writing Letters

Nonreaders or those on the beginning levels should be tested for their ability to write letters. The first phonics test, Letter Names, may be dictated to the student for this purpose. A complete inventory includes the ability to use manuscript letters in upper- and lowercase and, for more advanced students, the ability to write cursive letters in upper- and lowercase.

Handwriting: Writing Words in Sentences

Obtain a sample of the student's best effort. If one is not available, say, "*I would like to see your best handwriting. Please write what I say.*" Give the student lined paper appropriate in spacing to his or her age. A graded passage on the student's independent reading level may be used for dictation. Older students may be given a graded passage to copy in cursive writing. Use the handwriting section of the Written Language Expression Checklist (p. 133) to evaluate the student's effort.

Near- and Far-Point Copying

Ask students to copy passages on their highest independent reading levels from a distance of 10 or 12 feet and from a copy on their desk in front of them. They should copy different passages of the same length and difficulty. The examiner should record the time taken to copy each passage and should observe the number of letters and words copied after each glance, pointing behavior, auditorizing, and other indicators of difficulty or ease with the task. A comparison of time and behaviors for the two tasks may reveal problems in near-point or far-point vision. Memory span for written language may also be evaluated.

Writing from Dictation

This task may be used to evaluate the student's ability to remember spoken words and phrases in a meaningful context. Students with problems in this area may be able to write only one or two words at a time. As the examiner dictates the passage, he or she should observe the student's accuracy and adjust the number of words dictated accordingly.

Expressing Ideas in Writing

Obtain samples of the student's best efforts to express ideas in writing. If these are not available, give the student a picture (as in the Oral Language Assessment procedure) and ask him or her to write a story about it. Using the same device for evaluating written and oral language gives the examiner an opportunity to compare development. Usually a student's oral expression is better, but some students with retrieval problems may do better in written expression. Give the student unlimited time to write, but note the time taken to produce the story.

Use the Written Language Expression Checklist to evaluate the student's efforts. The student's general development in writing can be evaluated by preparing a file of several writing samples typical of students in each grade level and comparing products.

WRITTEN LANGUAGE EXPRESSION CHECKLIST

Yes	No	Comparison with Peers Indicates Satisfactory Performance in:	Descriptions and Examples of Problems
____	____	Copying letters	_____
____	____	Writing letters from dictation	_____
____	____	Writing sentences from dictation	_____

Handwriting

Yes	No		
____	____	Letter formation	_____
____	____	Proportion slant	_____
____	____	Rate of letter production	_____
____	____	Spacing letters, words, lines	_____
____	____	Legibility	_____

Syntactic Development

Yes	No		
____	____	Writing complete sentences	_____
____	____	Writing sentences of appropriate length and complexity	_____
____	____	Using correct grammar	_____

Mechanics

Yes	No		
____	____	Using capital letters	_____
____	____	Using punctuation	_____

Level of Abstraction

Yes	No		
____	____	Ability to describe concrete objects and actions	_____
____	____	Ability to present and discuss ideas	_____

Organization and Presentation of Ideas

Yes	No		
____	____	Coherence within sentences, paragraphs, total story, or essay	_____
____	____	Using organizational patterns: narrative, expository, sequence, cause-effect, comparison, contrast	_____
____	____	Using appropriate vocabulary	_____
____	____	Proofreading and correcting	_____
____	____	Other observations	_____

ARITHMETIC TEST

PURPOSE

An arithmetic test is included as a supplement to the battery for two reasons. First, the ability to perform basic arithmetic tasks is not dependent on reading. Students who do quite well in arithmetic, in contrast to reading, give evidence of their potential. The converse, of course, is not true. If a student does not do well in both reading and arithmetic, this does not mean potential is lacking but may indicate other underlying problems or simply a lack of instruction. Second, the writer of this test feels that remedial specialists and teachers should give assistance in all areas of essential needs such as reading, writing, spelling, and arithmetic. Overspecialization, leading to fragmentation in instruction, can result in the neglect of an area of basic functioning.

ADMINISTRATION

Give the student the test page and scrap paper to use. Say, *"Please work as many of these problems as quickly as you can. Be careful, but try not to waste time."* Allow 5 minutes, exactly! The test may be continued untimed after the problems that were finished have been noted. Additional answers obtained after 5 minutes are not to be included in the scoring but can be used to obtain further information. Observe the student's work unobtrusively.

The test may be given untimed. The grade level score is only an estimate. What is important is the student's ability to perform the operations.

SCORING AND INTERPRETATION

Total the number of right answers and refer to the Answer Key (p. 136) to obtain an estimate of level of performance. Note the categories of operations that the student understands. In addition, look for evidence of transposing or reversing numbers; consider whether the operation has been performed correctly even though the calculation was incorrect; look at rate in relation to accuracy; observe the student's need to verbalize; make tally marks; and so forth.

ARITHMETIC TEST

Score: _____ Grade Equiv.: _____ Name: _____

1. 3
   +4

2. 5
    3
   +4

3. 7
   −3

4. 12
   −5

5. 761
    543
   +123

6. 592
   −363

7. 7
   ×3

8. 402
   × 9

9. 4)$\overline{24}$

10. 9)$\overline{954}$

11. 5)$\overline{46}$

12. 32
   ×7

13. 7291
   −5460

14. 42
   ×73

15. 23)$\overline{1081}$

16. 7
   +2 $^1/_4$

17. $^1/_4$
   +$^3/_8$

18. 5 $^1/_2$
   −3

19. 7
   −4 $^2/_3$

20. $^2/_3$
     $^1/_2$
   +$^1/_6$

21. 371 $^3/_8$
   + 17 $^1/_4$

22. 16
   × 3 $^1/_4$

23. $^3/_4 \times ^2/_5 =$

24. $^3/_4 \div ^1/_2 =$

25. 37
   ×.04

26. .42
     .01
   +3.713

27. 7)$\overline{4.41}$

28. .07)$\overline{21.63}$

29. 29.1
   × 4.54

30. Write $^1/_4$
    as a
    decimal _____

ARITHMETIC TEST ANSWER KEY

1. 7	6. 229	11. 9.2	16. $9\frac{1}{4}$	21. $388\frac{5}{8}$	26. 4.143
2. 12	7. 21	12. 224	17. $\frac{5}{8}$	22. 52	27. .63
3. 4	8. 3618	13. 1831	18. $2\frac{1}{2}$	23. $\frac{3}{10}$	28. 309
4. 7	9. 6	14. 3066	19. $2\frac{1}{3}$	24. $1\frac{1}{2}$	29. 132.114
5. 1427	10. 106	15. 47	20. $\frac{8}{6}$ or $1\frac{1}{3}$	25. 1.48	30. .25

Raw Score (number right) and Grade Equivalent

Score	0	1	2	3	4	5	6	7	8	9	10	11	12
Grade	1.0	1.5	2.0	2.5	3.0	3.5	3.8	4.0	4.3	4.5	4.8	5.0	5.3

Score	13	14	15	16	17	18	19	20	21	22	23	24	25+
Grade	5.5	5.8	6.3	6.5	7.0	7.5	8.0	8.5	9.0	9.5	10.0	10.5	10.5+

Calculation Categories

simple addition: 1, 2, 5
addition of fractions: 16, 17, 20, 21
addition of decimals: 26
simple subtraction: 3, 4, 6, 13
subtraction of fractions: 18, 19
simple multiplication: 7, 8, 12, 14

multiplication of fractions: 22, 23
multiplication of decimals: 25, 29
simple division: 9, 10, 11, 15
division of fractions: 24
division of decimals: 27, 28
decimal conversion: 30

OPEN BOOK READING ASSESSMENTS

DESCRIPTION

Open book reading assessments (OBRAs) are informal silent reading assessments employing questions to be answered or tasks to be performed by the reader with the selection before her or him. The material is taken from academic material or daily-life reading. The skills tested by questions or tasks may reflect course goals or life competencies. OBRAs are most appropriate for those reading above the third-grade level. They may be used with individuals or with groups.

PURPOSES

The purposes of the open book tests are (1) to obtain specific information on students' abilities to understand and use content area, vocational, or daily-life reading materials; (2) to plan instruction; and (3) to confirm or supplement other diagnostic data.

CONSTRUCTION

1. Portions of material considered to be typical reading for the student within particular areas of emphasis should be selected. For content areas this might include textbooks, periodicals, or pamphlets; for vocational areas, manuals, indexes, or directories; and for other life-role areas, newspapers, schedules, and catalogs. Passage length will depend on the student's reading ability.
2. To determine the abilities to be evaluated, consider (a) the nature of the tasks to be performed with the material and the levels of comprehension required, and (b) the enabling skills required to perform the tasks or comprehend the information. With regard to tasks and levels, will the reader need to interpret graphs and maps? Follow directions? Identify summarizing or main-idea statements? Evaluate information? When the main objectives of using the material have been determined, the test constructor can then turn to the enabling objectives. For example, will the reader be able to understand the technical and general vocabulary? Skim to find specific items of information? To perceive the organization of the information?
3. Multiple choice, matching, or short-answer test items should be constructed. These will be easier to score, but, more importantly, they will evaluate the student's ability to understand what he has read rather than his ability to express himself (a higher level of functioning). This is not to say that expression should not be tested but that the underlying ability (comprehension) should be tested separately. In this way, the diagnostician can separate those students who comprehend but cannot express themselves verbally from those who cannot comprehend *and* cannot express themselves verbally.
4. Page and paragraph numbers should be provided for each question unless surveying or locational skills are being tested. The more items within a category, the more reliable the test. At least five or six items per category should be constructed. The test should be piloted on a sample of average readers, and poor items should be rewritten or discarded.
5. Separate writing assessments may evaluate the ability to summarize, to evaluate, and to relate information.

Sample categories and questions from various content areas:

Technical Vocabulary

1. fossil (page 232, paragraph 2)
   (a) A rock shaped by wind or water into the form of an animal
   (b) A trace of an animal or plant that lived long ago
   (c) A search for animals that lived in the Ice Age
   (d) A plan to reconstruct animals from the Ice Age
   (e) I don't know

2. composing room (page 24, paragraph 1)
   (a) Where news is set in type
   (b) Where news articles are written
   (c) Where news items are selected
   (d) Where news policy is established
   (e) I don't know

General Vocabulary

1. distinguish (page 52, paragraph 5)
   (a) Group together
   (b) Give a name
   (c) Tell apart
   (d) Find a total
   (e) I don't know
2. dwells (page 6, paragraph 6)
   (a) Eats
   (b) Dives
   (c) Walks
   (d) Lives
   (e) I don't know

Specific Context Clues to Vocabulary

1. coagulates (page 44). The acid thickens or *coagulates* the proteins of milk.
   (a) Makes a larger quantity
   (b) Makes more dense
   (c) Makes more digestible
   (d) Makes sour tasting
   (e) I don't know
2. opaque (page 42). You can see through glass, but wood is *opaque*.
   (a) Can't be melted
   (b) Can't break it
   (c) Can't be bent
   (d) Can't look through it
   (e) I don't know

Main Ideas

1. The main idea (important principle) on page 24 is:
   (a) Winds blow across the water.
   (b) Evaporation lowers the air temperature.
   (c) Moisture is removed from the air.
   (d) Refrigerators can help preserve food.
   (e) I don't know
2. The main idea (statement of theory) on page 110 is:
   (a) The United States is in the temperate zone.
   (b) Countries in temperate zones make greater progress.
   (c) Progress is measured by gross national product.
   (d) Climate affects the course of world history.
   (e) I don't know

Literal Details

1. Circle three examples of an amphibian (pages 31 and 32)
   (a) frog   (d) turtle   (g) salamander
   (b) bird   (e) toad   (h) water buffalo
   (c) fish   (f) alligator   (i) snake

2. The new stars of 1600 and 1604 were observed by (page 34)
   (a)   Galileo
   (b)   Copernicus
   (c)   Kepler
   (d)   Tycho Brahe
   (e)   I don't know

Interpretation

1. Match the following statements to the diagrams:

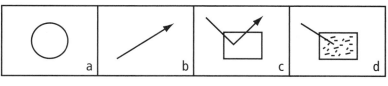

____ Light can be bent. (p. 42)

____ Light can be reflected. (p. 43)

____ Light travels in straight lines. (p. 42)

____ Light can be absorbed. (p. 44)

____ Light can travel through space. (p. 44)

2. Sam's mother appeared to be (pp. 82–84)
   (a) worried   (c) angry   (e) not concerned
   (b) disappointed   (d) pleased about his new job

Using Charts

1. Olefin is cleaned by (p. 59)
   (a)   washing in warm water
   (b)   washing in hot water
   (c)   dry cleaning
   (d)   brushing with cornstarch
   (e)   I don't know
2. The distance from Lansing to Central City is (see map grid)
   (a)   62 miles
   (b)   72 miles
   (c)   86 miles
   (d)   59 miles
   (e)   I don't know

Using Book Parts

In my textbook, to find quickly			I would turn to:	on page:
____	____	A definition of a technical word	(a) table of contents	(1) ii
____	____	Pages that mention a particular person's name	(b) preface	(2) 390
____	____	A statement of why the author wrote the book	(c) the glossary	(3) iii
____	____	Name of book's publisher	(d) title page	(4) vii
____	____	Outline of what is in the book	(e) index	(5) 385

ADMINISTRATION

Students should be given a generous amount of time, although those who take much longer than others should be noted as they may require further testing. The OBRA may be given in sections so that students who are unable to concentrate for a sustained period will not be inclined to guess or mark answers without reading the material. As with all test administration, students should be given clear, explicit instructions, encouraged to do their best, and observed for evidence of inattention to the task or confusion over test directions.

SCORING

As a general guide, 80 percent may be considered adequate for most categories. If several students are tested, the results might be charted as follows:

	Literal Details						Technical Vocabulary						Main Ideas						And so on
	1	2	3	4	5	6	7	8	9	10	11	12	13	14	15	16	17	18	
Jim	x	x		x	x		x	x		x	x	x			x		x		
Sue	x	x	x	x	x	x	x	x	x	x	x		x						
Donald	x	x		x						x	x						x		
Linda	x	x	x	x	x	x	x	x	x	x	x	x	x	x	x		x	x	
And so on																			

The number refers to the test item; an "x" indicates a correct answer.

ANALYSIS

An analysis of the results can provide information on specific strengths and weaknesses. If the chart is read vertically, it can reveal group needs; if read horizontally, it can indicate individual needs. Jim, for example, needs help in identifying main ideas in his textbooks, whereas Donald's low performance in one of the easier sections of the test, literal comprehension, suggests the need for further evaluation in the areas of general vocabulary and underlying concepts. If these are quite low, he should not be required to use this text. If these are satisfactory, Donald's listening comprehension of the material should be evaluated to see whether he can have the textbook read to him while instruction is provided to improve his technical vocabulary and comprehension.

Students should be given feedback on their performance. This can be done by photocopying the chart, cutting it into strips, and giving each student his or her results. Then the teacher can explain the reasoning processes and knowledge required by each category. This might be the first time some of the students have gotten any insights as to what their comprehension skills are and what kinds of reasoning need to be done to comprehend various kinds of printed matter.

The OBRA can be extended over grade levels by constructing additional tests for material on higher and lower grade levels. Donald might be evaluated on easier material, whereas Linda might be evaluated on more challenging material. Students have a level at which they can function fairly well, but within that level they have strengths and weaknesses.

The teacher can develop a file of OBRAs on materials on different levels in various areas over a period of time that can be used to supplement a diagnostic battery or to place students in materials.

PART 3

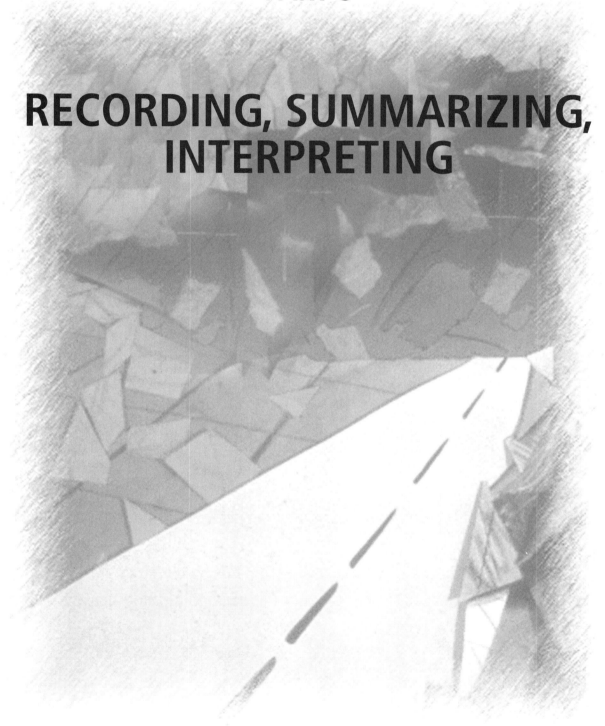

RECORDING, SUMMARIZING, INTERPRETING

STUDENT BACKGROUND INFORMATION

Forms are included to assist in the collection of background information, if it is available from home or the classroom teacher. The adult intake information form includes the adult interview and referral information.

Summarizing Assessment

The results of the student evaluation can be summarized on the Bader Reading and Language Inventory Summary Sheet (K–12) (see p. 148) or on the Bader Reading and Language Inventory Summary Sheet (Adult) (see p. 150). The K–12 form contains the following categories: reading profile, including instructional level and needs in reading; language development needs; instructional needs in spelling, handwriting, and arithmetic; visual and auditory difficulties; emergent literacy; student strengths, priorities, interests, and concerns; recommendations for instruction. The adult form contains information useful in tutoring for basic literacy and the English as a second language category.

Copies of relevant checklists or subtests of the inventory and other samples of the student's work can be stapled to the summary sheet in order to provide more specific information.

The examiner is encouraged to give as few or as many tests as seem to be appropriate. Finally, she or he should remember that recommendations for instruction should be made on all observations and information available, including the student's interests and attitudes as well as the instructional assistance that will be available. Whenever possible, trial teaching should be done to verify diagnosis and the selection of appropriate methods. Therefore, this assessment deemphasizes conclusions drawn from quantification of a few limited samples of behavior. Teachers and reading and learning specialists are encouraged to consider the student's abilities and needs from a holistic perspective.

BACKGROUND INFORMATION: K–12

Classroom Teacher's Referral Information

Student: _____

Teacher: _____

Grade: _____
      Year   Month

Age: _____
      Year   Month

1. Student's reading level: _____

2. Title of reading text or program: _____ Level: _____
   Supplementary material most frequently used

Title: _____ Level: _____

Title: _____ Level: _____

3. Reading abilities

    Word Identification

Strengths	Weaknesses		Comments
_____	_____	Semantic cues	_____
_____	_____	Syntactic cues	_____
_____	_____	Grapho-phonic cues	_____
_____	_____	Consonants	_____
_____	_____	Vowels	_____
_____	_____	Letter combinations	_____
_____	_____	Use of letter sound knowledge	_____
_____	_____	Sight vocabulary	_____
_____	_____	Phrasing	_____
_____	_____	Recognition of multisyllable words	_____

    Comprehension

Strengths	Weaknesses		Comments
_____	_____	Activates background knowledge	_____
_____	_____	Predicts	_____
_____	_____	Understands major concepts	_____
_____	_____	Self-monitors	_____
_____	_____	Recalls with prompts	_____
_____	_____	Recalls without prompts	_____
_____	_____	Interprets meaning suggested by the text	_____

4. Reading abilities

Strengths	Weaknesses	Comments
_____	_____ Spelling	_____
_____	_____ Handwriting	_____
_____	_____ Listening comprehension	_____
_____	_____ Study skills	_____
_____	_____ Oral expression	_____
_____	_____ Mathematics	_____
_____	_____ Written expression	_____

5. Has student received special help in reading? _____ When? _____

Nature of instruction? _____

Results? _____

6. Attitudes

Strengths	Weaknesses	Comments
_____	_____ Ability to concentrate	_____
_____	_____ Confidence in ability	_____
_____	_____ Willing to risk error	_____
_____	_____ Intent to remember	_____
_____	_____ Ability to work alone	_____
_____	_____ Enjoyment of material read aloud	_____

7. Interests _____

School _____

After school _____

Favorite books _____

8. Health

Strengths	Weaknesses	Nature of problem(s) if any
_____	_____ Vision	_____
_____	_____ Hearing	_____
_____	_____ Other	_____

9. Student strengths _____

10. Student weaknesses (other than reading) _____

11. Additional information you feel is important _____

CHILD'S HOME INFORMATION

Child's name: _____ Birthdate: _____

Address: _____ Phone: _____

Language(s) spoken in home: _____

Childhood diseases, serious injuries, surgery, and age at which each occurred: _____

_____

Does your child wear, or has she or he ever worn, glasses? _____

    If so, why? _____

When was your child's last vision check? _____

    Results? _____

Has your child had many ear infections? _____

Has your child had his/her hearing examined by a doctor? _____

Do you think your child hears well? _____

Does your child have any health problems? Explain. _____

When was your child last examined by a physician? _____

List any types of medication she or he is now receiving. _____

Do you feel your child has any speech or language problems? _____

    If so, describe. _____

Do you think your child misses too much school? _____

    Has your child ever missed school for long periods of time? If so, explain. _____

_____

What is your child's attitude toward school? _____

What are his/her best subjects? _____ Least successful subjects? _____

What is your child's attitude toward reading? _____

When was his/her difficulty with reading first noticed? _____

What do you think may be the cause of his/her reading problems? _____

Does your child read voluntarily? _____ What? _____

Are there reading materials in your home that are appropriate for your child? _____

Does your child spend time on his/her schoolwork at home? _____

Does your child have a quiet place to study? _____

Is there anyone at home who can help him/her read? _____

How much time does your child spend watching television? _____

How does your child get along with siblings? _____

    Others his/her age? _____ Parents? _____

What is his/her usual disposition? _____

Do you think your child gets enough rest? _____

    Does he or she become easily fatigued? _____

Does your child generally listen attentively when you talk to him/her? _____

Does he or she follow directions well? _____

Does your child generally see tasks through to completion? _____

How does he or she usually react to authority? _____

Are there situations in which your child becomes easily frustrated? _____

    If so, explain. _____

Please add any information that you feel will aid in understanding and helping your child.

_____

_____

Name of person completing form: _____

Relationship to child: _____

K–12 SUMMARY

Bader Reading and Language Inventory

Student's name: _____ School: _____ Date: _____

Grade in school: _____ Age: _____ Birthdate: _____ Examiner: _____

I. Reading Profile

Language development: Low: _____ Average: _____ High: _____

English as a second language: No: _____ Yes: _____ Level: _____

    Recommended level for instruction _____

    Recommended level for independent learning:

    _____ Word list

    _____ Oral reading

    _____ Silent reading comprehension

    _____ Listening comprehension

Instructional Needs in Reading

Word Recognition	*Comprehension*
_____ Semantic cues	_____ Prior knowledge
_____ Syntactic cues	_____ Prediction strategies
_____ Grapho-phonic cues	_____ Self-monitoring
_____ Consonant sounds	_____ Literal
_____ Vowel sounds	_____ Interpretive
_____ Blending	_____ Narrative
_____ Structural analysis	_____ Expository
_____ Automaticity	_____ Vocabulary
	_____ Rate

II. Language Development Needs

_____ Receptive language	_____ Written expression
_____ English as a second language	_____ Conceptual development
_____ Oral expression	_____ Vocabulary development

III. Other Instructional Needs

_____ Spelling _____ Handwriting _____ Arithmetic

IV. Visual-Auditory Difficulties

___ Visual acuity   ___ Auditory acuity

___ Visual discrimination   ___ Auditory discrimination

V. Preliteracy

___ Language awareness   ___ Hearing letters in words

___ Blending   ___ Matching words in sentences

___ Segmenting   ___ Comprehending stories

___ Letter knowledge

VI. Student Strengths

_____

_____

VII. Student Priorities, Interests, Concerns

_____

_____

VIII. Summary of Recommendations for Instruction

_____

_____

_____

_____

_____

_____

_____

ADULT-LEVEL SUMMARY

Bader Reading and Language Inventory

Student's name: _____ Staff: _____ Date: _____

1. Reading level: _____ (word list: _____ passages: _____)

2. Language comprehension: appears low _____ , average _____ , high _____ , ESL _____

3. Instructional needs:

   _____ Alphabet   _____ Multisyllabic words

   _____ Name   _____ Vocabulary

   _____ Write   _____ Spelling*

   _____ Sight words   _____ Rate

   _____ Consonant sounds   _____ Writing

   _____ Vowel patterns   _____ Study skills

   _____ Letter combinations   _____ Math

   _____ Use of context   _____ Other _____

   _____ Use of phonics

   Sight words recognized (primer level and below only): _____

   _____

4. Student strengths: _____

   _____

5. Student goals, interests, concerns: _____

   _____

   _____

6. Suggestions for materials or methods: _____

   _____

   _____

   _____

   _____

   _____

*Note: Please attach spelling paper to back of this form.

7. Tutoring times available: Day _____ and Evening _____ _____

    Geographical preference

           City: _____ N _____ S _____ W _____ E _____

    Near home: _____

    Flexible: _____

    Have tutoring site to suggest: _____

    Other: _____

    Have transportation? Yes _____ No _____

    Notes:

THE ADULT LIFE-ROLE PORTFOLIO

   After discussion with each student to determine the portfolio purposes, write the purposes as the student dictates them; then, discuss how the portfolio will be organized, where it will be kept, who will have access to it, how it will be used, and other concerns of the student to her or his satisfaction. Purposes and plans may be adjusted over time.

A suggested way to organize the portfolio is to have sections on:

READING FOR ENJOYMENT AND INFORMATION.*   The student may keep a log of articles and books, as in this example:

Date	Title	New Ideas/Words	Comments

Tapes of the student's reading may be made to demonstrate growth. The student can also be helped to make a list of topics and specific titles of books and magazines for future reading.

DOCUMENT READING AND WRITING.*   The teacher and student collect materials basic to daily life needs and interests. Here are some examples.

   Transportation: road signs; bus, train, and subway signs; destinations on vehicles; maps; schedules; and driver's manuals

   Food: Package labels, directions for preparation, recipes, menus

   Health: directions on prescriptions and over-the-counter medications, directions for follow-up, home medical care, infant and child care, health history forms

   Workplace: want ads, job applications, memos from supervisors, simple computer entries, time slips, performance indicators, job outlines, agreements

   Safety: danger and warning signs, instructions to operate appliances and equipment

   Assistance and information: telephone book, newspaper, directories

   The student chooses the items he or she wants to master and sets priorities for study with the teacher's help. Lists may be kept of words to learn to read and write for each item. A log may be kept of documents mastered. A copy of the most important, correctly completed forms should be given to the student for his or her use.

   QUANTITATIVE READING AND WRITING.*   Procedures are followed as in the preceding section. Materials may include bills, checks, bank statements, loan agreements, rental agreements, warranties, guarantees, tax forms, advertisements, social security forms, price tags, order forms, and refund and discount information.

   PERSONAL, BUSINESS, AND CREATIVE WRITING.   The student chooses the kinds of writing most important to him or her: letters and notes to friends, family, and the child's teacher; an autobiography; letters requesting information or assistance and letters to the editor; poems, stories, essays, scripts, and journals; ideas for future projects; photo album notations; and baby books.

   ORAL AND NONVERBAL LANGUAGE.   The student chooses areas of importance: polite social and business greetings and exchanges, giving and receiving directions, explaining, requesting, and imagining. Evidence of growth may be documented by tapes, checklists, and anecdotal reports.

*Areas selected for evaluation of literacy in the 1992 National Adult Literacy Survey sponsored by the U.S. Department of Education.

STUDENT SELF-EVALUATIONS. Based on her or his goals, the student selects areas to evaluate and notes progress with the teacher's help. Take care to examine only one or two elements at a time and celebrate achievements.

USING STANDARDS DOCUMENTS IN PORTFOLIOS

Portfolio contents may be used to demonstrate achievement of district, state, or national standards and goals. For example, a student's reading log may help meet the standard of "reading a variety of genres for enjoyment." A student's social studies report may help meet the standard of "synthesizing information from several sources." State departments of education and school districts have developed goal standards and benchmark documents that may be obtained for adoption or adaptation.

RECOMMENDED READING

Cooper, C., & Odell, L. (Eds.). (1977). *Evaluating writing.* Champaign, IL: National Council of Teachers of English.

NAEP Reading Consensus Project. (1992). *Reading framework for the 1992 national assessment of educational progress.* Washington, D.C.: U.S. Government Printing Office.

National Institute for Literacy. [On-line]. Available: http://novel.nifl.gov/

Tierney, R. J., Carter, M. A., & Desai, L. E. (1991). *Portfolio assessment in the reading and writing classroom.* Norwood, VA: Christopher Gordon Publishers.

Wolf, D. P. (1989). "Portfolio assessment: Sample student work." *Educational Leadership, 46,* 35–39.

Yancy, K. B. (Ed.). (1992). *Portfolios in the writing classroom.* Champaign, IL: National Council of Teachers of English.

CASE STUDY: JACKIE

Michelle Johnston presents the following case study to illustrate the reasoning of a reading diagnostician as he or she uses the Bader Reading and Language Inventory to assess a child's reading needs and make recommendations for instruction.

GETTING STARTED

Ms. Irving referred Jackie to the school district reading diagnostician during March of her second grade. When Mr. Frank, the diagnostician, reviewed Ms. Irving's reasons for referring Jackie for a reading diagnosis (see Classroom Teacher's Referral Information Form), examined her cumulative records, observed her classroom performance, and interviewed her mother (see Child's Home Information form), he discovered that her reading difficulties were not new. In fact, Jackie had a history of delayed language acquisition, apparent difficulties learning various reading conventions in kindergarten and first grade, and comprehension problems. However, according to her mother, her current teacher, Ms. Irving, and her previous teacher, her reading difficulties did not appear to be severe earlier. But as the reading materials became more complex, she exhibited increasing levels of difficulty and frustration. Mr. Frank also found that Jackie moved twice in kindergarten and once near the end of first grade in addition to missing a significant amount of second grade. She has attended Wilson Elementary since late April of first grade; therefore, her first grade teacher noted some difficulties but indicated that she really did not have time to investigate those difficulties in late May and June.

HOME AND FAMILY RESOURCES

Jackie's mother was concerned about her reading progress, but as a single parent who worked evenings and supported four children without any other financial assistance, she did not have time to work with Jackie. Her mother reported that a grandmother helped with babysitting and child care, but there were not extra resources in the family to afford many books or programs such as summer reading programs between first and second grades or, looking ahead, between second and third. However, she was willing to figure out some at-home tutoring program and thought that the grandmother or a cousin could help.

RULING OUT PROBLEMS AND DEVELOPING A DIAGNOSTIC PLAN

Because Mr. Frank was concerned about Jackie's reported language delay and her difficulty in learning reading conventions, including phonics, he decided to rule out any physical issues that would interfere with her reading progress. Therefore, with the help of the school nurse and speech/language consultant, he recommended thorough vision, hearing, and language screenings. While he waited for the results of the screenings, Mr. Frank met with Jackie and began the Bader Reading and Language Inventory with an interview, using the Student Priorities and Interests form. He found her to be energetic and positive, but aware that she was not reading as well as the other students in her class. Although Jackie liked listening to stories and reading predictable books, she appeared to be embarrassed about her reading skills and lacked confidence. In making decisions about his diagnostic strategies, Mr. Frank integrated the research findings from Snow et al. (1996) regarding the prevention of reading difficulties with the Bader Reading and Language Inventory to formulate his diagnostic plan (see Flowcharts). Specifically, he determined that once he knew her reading level, he would also rule out the following difficulties: phonemic awareness, motor development, letter identification, automatic response, visual, verbal, and aural processing, and language development. Therefore, he started with the preprimer word list (PP) and found her instructional level using the word lists to be at the primer (P) level.

By the time Mr. Frank completed Jackie's interview and presented the word lists to her, the nurse and speech/language consultant were ready to share their findings. Jackie's vision and hearing were normal; however, the speech/language consultant felt that her oral language was somewhat low for her age level. She was especially concerned about her vocabulary development. Therefore, she went beyond her usual work with Jackie and investigated her understanding of concepts where, again, Jackie appeared to be performing slightly below most children her age. From the conference with the other two specialists, Mr. Frank began formulating Jackie's reading profile with the following decision: he would recommend that the speech/language consultant would work with Ms. Irving to select activities to improve Jackie's concept and vocabulary/language development.

ANALYZING READING ABILITIES

Using her performance on the word lists as a guide, Mr. Frank invited Jackie to begin reading the oral paragraphs at the primer level. Her oral reading performance, including accuracy and recall, was at the first grade level. However, she read deliberately, word-by-word. She recognized punctuation and exhibited unaided recall of the information at the literal level. When she did not know a word, she did not attempt to decode or identify the word through context clues. Therefore, the unknown words interfered with her ability to read orally and understand the passages. When Mr. Frank asked her to read silently, she whispered the words in the passage and did not read silently. Mr. Frank noted that Jackie's listening comprehension was on the second grade level. He added the following information to Jackie's reading profile to share with Ms. Irving and her mother: recommended level for instruction, first grade; independent reading level, primer; listening comprehension, second grade; comprehension appeared to be literal, not interpretive.

Mr. Frank was optimistic because Jackie could listen to second grade level passages and understand them. He told her mother and teacher that her listening comprehension indicated that she could make progress once he figured out the difficulties that were impeding her progress. He recommended that they read to her, talk about the stories they were reading, have her read to them, and start finding interesting words in the stories and environment to discuss. To move her comprehension to an interpretive level, he encouraged them to have her create different story endings, ask "why" questions, and think about "what if" scenarios with the stories they read. Additionally, he asked Jackie to start writing a journal to record interesting ideas from stories and words that she either saw or heard spoken to share with others.

Mr. Frank suggested that her mother and teacher read in unison with her and that her teacher include choral reading as a reading instructional activity. Through reading in unison and choral reading, Jackie could develop fluency and eventually read more smoothly.

Spending some time independently reading high interest books on the primer level would contribute to instant word recognition, fluency, and enjoyment of reading.

Jackie liked to read about animals, particularly cats. Easy-to-read books about cats were easy to find.

FINDING SPECIFIC NEEDS

Before Mr. Frank gave Jackie the Diagnostic Spelling Tests, he asked Jackie to bring samples of her writing to the next session and requested that Ms. Irving also share Jackie's writing samples. He was interested in finding patterns of errors that would give him clues about Jackie's phonetic and visual acuity. After analyzing her performance on the Diagnostic Spelling Test, Mr. Frank determined that Jackie's estimated performance was on the preprimer level. She seemed to recognize beginning and ending sounds represented by single consonants in words but had difficulty with middle sounds; she rarely made substitutions. Therefore, he decided to use the Visual Discrimination Tests and Auditory Discrimination Test in the Preliteracy Testing Record to get to the underlying problem.

Remarkably, Jackie did well on the Visual Discrimination Tests, ruling out visual discrimination problems that interfered with her reading progress. However, her performance on the Auditory Discrimination Test was problematic, indicating the need for additional assessment of her phonemic awareness and knowledge of phonics. Mr. Frank moved the diagnosis forward, skipping Literacy Concepts because he knew Jackie had a good understanding of the concepts, to the other subtests examining phonic elements. He omitted consonant testing, because she demonstrated her knowledge in her spelling test. He found that she did not know many of the vowel sounds and had difficulty with blending and segmenting.

Jackie demonstrated that her use of syntactic and semantic cues were appropriate for her age.

Language processing did not appear to be a problem.

SUMMARIZING THE FINDINGS AND MAKING RECOMMENDATIONS

After pinpointing some issues related to phonemic manipulation and phonics, Mr. Frank felt that he was prepared to complete his summary of Jackie's instructional needs. Although he was uncertain of the causes for her reading difficulties, he made several conjectures. He thought that her moving in kindergarten and first grade might have interfered with her progress. Perhaps the school districts were not consistent in their teaching of reading fundamentals, or Jackie's own adjustment to the new schools may have been problematic. Mr. Frank also thought Jackie probably did not practice reading enough to habituate it. Therefore, his summary of her instructional needs included:

1. Ensuring that Jackie has lots of practice reading high interest books
2. Developing competencies using grapho-phonic cues, segmenting, and blending by integreting oral language, reading, and writing activities
3. Engaging prior knowledge and prediction strategies to develop her self-monitoring capabilities
4. Exposing her to varieties of texts in different genres that would enhance her interpretive comprehension
5. Expanding her vocabulary (word meaning) through concept development
6. Building a repertoire of fix-up strategies to use when she encounters unknown words
7. Embedding phonics instruction in context and in spelling

Because Jackie is at the end of second grade, Mr. Frank found a tutor for her and a free summer program with trained teachers or tutors, possibly from Volunteers for Service to America or America Reads. A senior citizen volunteer tutor contacted by Mr. Frank and a neighbor of Jackie's family offered to work with her twice a week and walk her to the library. Mr. Frank felt that Jackie could make good progress if this intensive help could continue through third grade.

CASE ANALYSIS

Many children like Jackie, who move frequently in their early schooling, miss the fundamentals of beginning reading instruction. Additionally, without access to children's books and sufficient practice reading, they do not habituate reading and develop fluency. Because Jackie was at the end of second grade, Ms. Irving and Mr. Frank had a daunting task. They had to ensure that she would enter third grade reading and writing successfully. According to Snow, Burns, and Griffin (1998), when children do not learn to read by third grade, reading problems tend to plague them throughout their schooling because, in third grade and beyond, the focus moves from learning to read to reading to learn.

Mr. Frank provides a good example of a reading diagnostician by following organized diagnostic procedures. First, he ruled out vision, hearing, and language problems by seeking expert consultation and assistance and by gaining a thorough understanding of Jackie's reading problems by checking records and interviewing her teachers and parent. Second, Mr. Frank formulated his plan based on sound theory and research. Third, as he gained information about Jackie, he shared it with the teacher and her mother, making recommendations for correction as he progressed through the diagnosis. Fourth, he combined samples of classroom work in spelling and writing with testing and skipped diagnosis subtests on which he knew she could succeed.

Ms. Irving was fortunate to have access to someone like Mr. Frank. However, if there were no reading diagnosticians available through her school district, Ms. Irving could have completed the Bader Reading and Language Inventory as part of a classroom assessment strategy, making observations and giving subtests over a couple of weeks. Although in-depth testing takes time, usually only a few children in each classroom need such a close look. With an understanding of their strengths and needs, they can succeed.

REFERENCE

Snow, C. E., Burns, M. S.,& Griffin, P. (Eds.). (1998). Preventing reading difficulties in young children. Washington, DC: National Academy Press. [On-line]. Available: http://books.nap.edu/html/prdyc/

PART 4

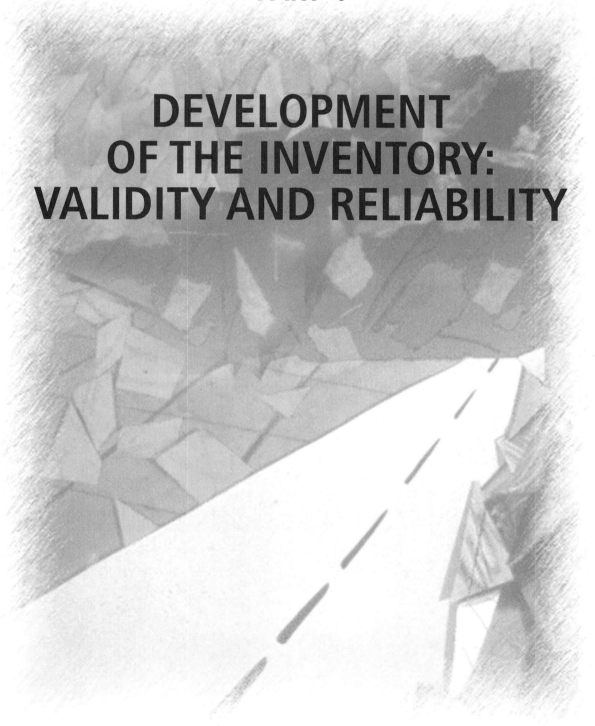

DEVELOPMENT
OF THE INVENTORY:
VALIDITY AND RELIABILITY

DEVELOPING AND VALIDATING THE INVENTORY

The selection and development of the tasks in the Inventory are based on several years of experience in individual assessment of elementary, secondary, and adult learners and on the basis of a careful analysis of research and authoritative opinion in the literature. All parts of the battery have been tested with the aid of experienced reading specialists on K-12 and adult levels with at least a master's degree in reading. Since the publication of the first edition, professors with doctorates in reading, special education, and speech and language have used the battery in preparing teachers and reading and language specialists, and in conducting research; they have endorsed its content and procedures. Fitzgerald (2001) explained in the *Reading Research Quarterly* that she used the Bader Reading and Language Inventory in her study "... because grade-level equivalents of passages of the published inventory are well established and because, unlike some other inventories, early reading levels are represented in both preprimer and primer passages, providing greater sensitivity to initial reading levels."

THE GRADED WORD LIST

One purpose of the graded word list is to determine entry level for the graded passages. Words were selected from graded sight-word lists and readers that appeared to be appropriate for each level. The graded word list was tested by having reading specialists record the instructional level at which they had placed their students with mild to severe difficulties after diagnosis and trial teaching. Dr. Lonnie McIntyre, a professor at the University of Tennessee, compared students' scores on the Bader word list and the Slosson Oral Reading Test and found a correlation of 0.92. Similar results were found by Dr. Janet Dynak, a professor at Western Michigan University.

THE GRADED READING PASSAGES

The graded passages were either written by the author or selected from materials that appeared to be typical for the grade-level designations. Because research and experience indicate that performance is affected by the reader's attitude toward the content, passages were written or adapted that would be suitable for the maturity of the readers. Because the major purpose of graded passage assessment is to place students in graded materials, an attempt was made to create or to select and adapt materials similar to those in which the student might be placed. Therefore, one set of materials (C) was developed for children in or near the grade-level designation of the passages, a second set (C/A) was developed for use with either children or adults, and a third set (A) was developed for adults.

Questions were constructed to be as passage-dependent as possible. Because recall is being tested as well as understanding, questions are literal. To avoid problems with passage dependency, inferential reasoning is tested apart from literal recall and is not counted in the total score. The Bader Inventory uses retelling as a way of assessing perception of organizational structure and as a less stressful, more efficient way of testing. Gillet and Temple (1990) and Alexander and Heathington (1988) recommend this procedure and cite the Bader Inventory as one of the few commercial tests using retelling.

An insufficient number of passages are read in graded reading passage testing to use categories such as vocabulary, organization, inference, and main idea in a reliable way (Spache, 1981; Schell and Hanna, 1981). Because of the insufficient number of passages read to provide an estimate of the level of functioning, no attempt was made to differentiate significantly the passages by organizational structure or type of text. Most readers will have better recall of narrative passages than expository passages. Students' performance on both kinds of passages may be compared by selecting readings across C, C/A, and A sections of the inventory. Diagnosticians using the first edition of this inventory reported that student interest in the passages was much greater than their interest in comparable test passages. Dr. Larry Kenney (1996), a professor at the University of Wisconsin—Whitewater, asked students to read and compare passages from several published reading inventories and rank them as to interest and appeal. He reported that the Bader passages were ranked first, unanimously. Because interest strongly affects performance, this is the critical factor in more accurately estimating levels of functioning.

Readability was estimated with the Harris-Jacobson formula and the Fry formula. However, final adjustment of word selection and sentence length was made on overall content rather than on artificial manipulation.

Primarily to test the content, 30 elementary students, 20 secondary students, and 20 students in adult education read the passages. Passages that were not considered appealing were dropped.

Next, passages were tested for equivalence. Forty elementary students read C and C/A passages. Oral reading yielded a product-moment coefficient of 0.80, and silent reading yielded a correlation coefficient of 0.78. Forty secondary and adult students read C/A and A passages. The oral reading coefficient was 0.83, and the silent reading was 0.79. Fifteen older elementary students who were embarrassed by their poor reading ability were given the adult passages to examine these passages' effect on attitude. Response was positive with regard to the students' liking the content of the passages. However, no statistical evaluation was attempted.

A study was conducted by Dr. Daniel Pearce (1981), a professor at Texas A&M University, to examine the validity of the graded passages as an instrument for determining reading level. Thirty students in grades four through eight were administered the graded passages, and an instructional level was determined for every student. Next, each student's reading teacher was asked for the grade level for basal reader materials in which the student was receiving instruction. These teacher assessments were compared to the instructional level score obtained from the graded passages.

Bader and McIntyre (1986) compared the placements of 27 children, grades one through five, with diverse ethnic and racial backgrounds from low-income families. University students were given a two-hour workshop on administering the graded word list and oral and silent reading passages. They estimated a reading level that Dr. McIntyre compared to the reading levels determined by the school reading specialist and confirmed by the classroom teachers. The correlation was 0.93.

The adult passages, word lists, and spelling tests have been used with well over 4,000 functionally illiterate adults from 1989 to 2000 by the LVA, Capital Area Literacy Coalition in Lansing, Michigan, as well as by other literacy groups nationwide. These passages have been found to be acceptable to the adult students and to provide reliable indications of their literacy functioning. Since 1990, more than 6,000 children have been tested in LVA-CALC programs with high accuracy in comparison with school assessment.

The director of Project READ, Redwood City, California, Kathy Endaya (1997) reported that more than 1,800 adults, youth, and children have been assessed with the *Bader Reading and Language Inventory* since 1989. To continuously check the accuracy of its results from administration of the Bader Inventory, Project READ compares its assessment composite with learning specialists' results at Sequoia High School, Menlo-Atherton High School, and Fair Oaks Elementary School. Endaya states, "The Bader assessment results have continued to be consistently within half a reading level of the schools' total composite of tests. Further verification of the composite comes from reading and learning specialists at the Foster City Reading and Learning Institute. . . ."

With regard to evaluating rate with comprehension, Bond, Tinker, Wasson, and Wasson (1994) state that it appears to be hazardous to specify average rates for different grade levels. Rate varies with the kind of material, student background, and purpose for reading. Therefore, the examiner should test several good and poor readers in a specific reading situation to obtain data as to whether a student reads *relatively* slow or fast. The following grade-level norms, developed by Taylor, Frankenpohl, and Pettee (1960), have provided a good referent in the experience of the writer. However, all grade norms must be used with caution.

Grade:	1	2	3	4	5	6	7	8	9	10	11	12	college
Rate with comprehension:	80	115	138	158	173	185	195	204	214	224	227	250	280

Examiners may obtain a rate-per-minute estimate by using a stopwatch to time the student's reading and dividing the time into the total number of words (exclusive of title) listed at the end of each passage. However, most examiners would probably do better only to note extremely fast or slow reading.

Although the definitions for *instructional level* and *independent learning level* are given in another section, further explanation is indicated for their use. For several years the writer attempted to follow the standard informal reading inventory (IRI) guidelines in much of the literature. Students were usually placed in materials that were found to be too easy . Although one can rationalize placement in easy materials for the legitimate purposes of building fluency and confidence, the placements were often not appropriate for direct instruction. Research on the problems of determination of instructional level through IRIs suggests the need for revision of the classic, stringent requirements of word-for-word accuracy and the need to weigh comprehension.

The general guidelines for reading levels are as follows: The *instructional level* is one where students comprehend at least 75 percent of what they read and can recall at least 60 percent. Students may be considered to be at a *frustration level* when they exhibit behavioral indications of stress, miss more than 10 percent of the words, and understand less than 60 percent of what they read. Students may be considered at an *independent level* when they miss no more than 5 percent of the words, read fluently, and comprehend at least 80 percent of what they read. Please consider these as general guidelines. The purposes of the graded passages are (1) to find the highest instructional level at which the student can comprehend, and (2) to analyze reading to discover student strengths and problems in reading so that the student can be appropriately placed in materials for instruction. Little seems to be gained by computing frustration and independent levels.

Finally, one cannot ignore widespread classroom teaching practices. Many teachers place students in readers and auxiliary materials that require the student to do a great deal of independent work. Although one may question the value of some of these materials, students do use them and need to be placed in them about one level below their highest instructional level unless they are given direct instruction and support by their teacher. This is the *independent learning level.*

The Inventory provides a window on the reading process ".... so that affective, perceptual, linguistic and cognitive aspects of reading can be observed" (Bader and Wiesendanger, 1989). It has potential for training prospective teachers about reading behavior, unequaled by other types of learning, and it allows a close match between testing and teaching.

OTHER INVENTORY SUBTESTS AND CHECKLISTS

Remaining parts of the battery should be selected and interpreted according to the need of the student to perform the task (i.e., complete mastery or in terms of a comparison with peers). When research has suggested cutoff points, these have been recommended.

Carolyn Humphrey-Cummings (1982) administered the inventory graded paragraph test and word list test to 123 kindergarten students to determine if they were readers or nonreaders. Next, those reading were classified as decoders, sight readers, context users, or combination readers by analyzing their performance during paragraph reading and their ability to complete the Semantic Cloze Sentences, read nonsense words from the phonics inventory, and read sight words. These groups were administered five of the Inventory subtests that measured readiness abilities: naming letters, hearing letter names, syntax matching, writing letters, and spelling. All five of the subtests discriminated readers from nonreaders. Syntax matching was a significant task for all types of beginning readers. Syntax matching and spelling discriminated between readers using phonetic analysis and all other readers. Syntax matching and naming letters discriminated between sight readers and context readers. Bader and Hildebrand (1991) extended research on emergent literacy by administering selected inventory tasks to children ages three to five to study prereading concept development.

Although phonemic discrimination and phonemic manipulation are not new areas of concern in beginning reading, they are getting a great deal of attention. Researchers are not in agreement about which abilities predict success in reading. There is some evidence that phonemic awareness is acquired by some beginning readers as a consequence of learning to read (International Reading Association, 1998). When children have had instruction in beginning reading and continue to struggle, they may have difficulties in segmenting phonemes or in other language areas. If these problems cannot be overcome, they will need to be taught with approaches that do not depend on these skills or processes.

The ability to read and respond to various texts can be probed more validly during trial teaching or classroom instruction than in the relatively brief time allotted for testing. The diagnostician is encouraged to construct open-book reading tasks (Bader, 1980) or to use informal instructional sessions to assess abilities in academic or work-place areas for older children and adults. Guidelines for constructing open-book reading tasks are in this edition, but open-ended discussions that reflect the purposes of the reader are encouraged.

The English as a Second Language Quick Start Test and Checklist have been used with more than 2,000 refugees, immigrants, and migrant farm workers and their families served by the Literacy Volunteers of America, Capital Area Literacy Coalition. The Quick Start test provides a reliable guide to program and materials placement and gives administrators, teachers, and tutors a way to communicate about and report levels of proficiency. The checklist is arranged in a sequence frequently used by tutors and was validated by teachers at the Corporation for National Service, Volunteers in Service to America working with the Coalition.

REFERENCES AND SUGGESTED READINGS

References in this section include early classic discussions of assessment issues as well as newer publications and Inventory reviews.

Alexander, J. E., & Heathington, B. S. (1988). *Assessing and correcting classroom reading problems.* Glenville, IL: Scott, Foresman.

Bader, L. A. (1980). *Reading diagnosis and remediation in classroom and clinic.* New York: Macmillan.

Bader, L. A., & Hildebrand, V. (1991). An exploratory study of three to five year olds' responses on the Bader reading and language inventory to determine developmental stages of emerging literacy. *Early Child Development and Care, 77.*

Bader, L. A., & McIntyre, L. D. (1986, Fall). Improving reading through university and public school cooperation. *Journal of Children and Youth, 7.*

Bader, L. A., & Wiesendanger, K. (1989, Fall). Realizing the potential of informal reading inventories. *Journal of Reading, 32.*

Bond, G. L., Tinker, M. A., Wasson, B. B., & Wasson, J. B. (1994). *Reading difficulties.* Boston: Allyn and Bacon.

Cooter, R. B. (1990). *The teachers' guide to reading tests.* Scottsdale, AZ: Gorsuch Scaresborg Publishers.

Endaya, K. (1997). Bader reading and language inventory: Verification studies. Unpublished manuscript. Project READ. Redwood City Public Library, Redwood City, CA.

Fahey, K. B. (1996). Books/software reviews: Bader reading and language inventory. *ASHA Leader,.*

Fitzgerald, J. (2001). "Can minimally trained college student volunteers help young at-risk children read bettter?" *Reading Research Quarterly, 36,* 28–46.

Gillet, J. W., & Temple, C. (1990). *Understanding reading problems: Assessment and instruction.* Glenview, IL: Scott, Foresman/Little Brown Higher Education.

Harris, A. J., & Sipay, E. R. (1990). *How to increase reading ability,* 9th ed. New York: Longman.

Henderson, E. H., & Beers, J. W. (Eds.). (1980). *Developmental and cognitive aspects of learning to spell.* Newark, DE: International Reading Association.

Humphrey-Cummings, C. (1982). Differences in the acquisition of selected readiness abilities between readers and nonreaders in kindergarten. Ph.D. dissertation, Michigan State University.

International Reading Association. (1998). Phonemic awareness and the teaching of reading. Position statement from the Board of Directors of the International Reading Association.